A·Q·U·A·M·A·S

Peter Hisco

COMMUNITY FISH

BOWTIE
P R E S S®

A Division of BowTie, Inc.
Irvine, California

First published in the USA and Canada by
BowTie Press®
A Division of BowTie, Inc.
3 Burroughs
Irvine, CA 92618
www.bowtiepress.com

Originally published in 2007
© 2007 Interpet Publishing
Vincent Lane, Dorking, Surrey
RH4 3YX, England

Library of Congress Cataloging-in-Publication
Hiscock, Peter.
  Community fish / by Peter Hiscock.
     p. cm. — (Aquamaster)
  ISBN-13: 978-1-933958-07-1
  ISBN-10: 1-933958-07-3
  1. Aquarium fishes. 2. Aquariums. 3. Fish
communities. I. Title.

  SF457H575 2007
  639.34—dc22

2006100553

Created and compiled: Ideas into Print,
Claydon, Suffolk, IP6 0AB, England.
Design and prepress: Stuart Watkinson,
Ayelands, Longfield, Kent DA3 8JW, England.
Computer graphics: Stuart Watkinson.
Principal photography: Geoffrey Rogers
[copyright symbol] Interpet Publishing (also see
Picture credits page 96).
Production management: Consortium,
Poslingford, Suffolk CO10 8RA, England.
Print Production: Sino Publishing House Ltd.,
Hong Kong.

Printed and bound in China
10 9 8 7 6 5 4 3 2 1

Additional material supplied by Nick Fletcher,
Derek Lambert, Pat Lambert, Dick Mills, Gina
Sandford, Stuart Thraves

Contents

Natural habitats

In nature, fish can be found in virtually every water system. The tropical freshwater fish commonly kept by hobbyists are from a wide variety of areas spanning the entire globe. In all these areas, there are various habitats that are unique in style. These can also change dramatically throughout the year. Tropical freshwater fish have evolved to cope with such changes, which makes them ideal for aquariums. It does not mean that they will tolerate bad conditions, just that they have a better capacity to cope with change.

▲ *White Cloud Mountain minnows, fast-water fish*

Mountain streams are cool and fast flowing and are home to fish with streamlined bodies and short fins that can withstand the strongest currents. Many are algae eaters that can graze food from the rocks.

Some lakes in tropical regions develop through annual river flooding and may dry up within a few months. Other lakes are permanent, such as the African Rift Valley lakes, and provide a year-round habitat for many types of fish.

▲ *African Rift Valley Lake cichlids*

▶ *The rummy-nose tetra (Hemigrammus bleheri) lives in tropical rivers thick with plants.*

In tropical regions, the river may pass through dense rain forests that provide a wealth of food, including forest fruits and seeds. In the rainy season, the river bursts its banks, flooding the surrounding land.

Once a few tributaries have joined the main river, it becomes a wide expanse of water that can support a population of larger fish and animals. Depending on the location, the center of the river may be home to barbs, cichlids, catfish, and carp species that can reach 3.3 ft (1 m) in length.

▲ The large plecostomus (Hypostomus spp.) are suited to a fast-flowing river environment.

Swamps in lowland tropical habitats fluctuate in size with the floods and the dry seasons. The shallow water is crammed with vegetation and is home to many fish species, many of which have adapted to the murky, low-oxygen waters. Many bottom-dwelling catfish and loaches rely on touch and smell to locate their prey.

▲ Pearl gouramis (Trichogaster leeri) feel at home in a densely planted tank.

▶ The archerfish (Toxotes jaculatrix) does well in brackish water.

* Over time, rivers erode the surrounding land and change course, leaving pockets of water that may become pools, lakes, or lagoons.

As the river reaches the ocean, it begins to mix with saltwater, creating brackish habitats. Brackish fish have adapted to cope with the changing concentrations of salt in the water. In many tropical areas, mangrove swamps flourish in the brackish waters.

How fish live

As a fish keeper, it helps to become familiar with the names of the fins and other parts of the body. When you look at a fish, your first impressions of its body shape, the position of the fins, the size of the mouth, and the barbels (if present) can be very clear indicators of where in the water column the fish lives, whether it is sedentary or active, what it may or may not eat—and even whether it would be a safe addition to a community aquarium or whether it will eat everything else in it!

CYPRINIDS (DANIOS, BARBS, RASBORAS)

The cyprinids, such as this danio, are streamlined for fast movement and require open spaces in the aquarium.

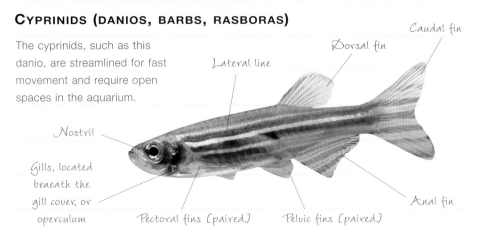

Caudal fin

Dorsal fin

Lateral line

Nostril

Gills, located beneath the gill cover, or operculum

Pectoral fins (paired)

Pelvic fins (paired)

Anal fin

SUCKERMOUTH CATFISH

▲ Like other suckermouth catfish, Hypostomus *has stout fin spines and three rows of bony plates along its body for protection. Take care when handling these fish, as they may become entangled in the net. Do not attempt to pull a fish free; either let it free itself or carefully cut away the net.*

* *Some catfish have locking pectoral fin spines that anchor the fish to objects and are a valuable form of defense.*

SURFACE-DWELLING FISH

▲ *The flat back and upturned mouth of the sparkling panchax 'Golden Wonder'* (Aplocheilus lineatus) *are typical of fish that live and feed at the water's surface.*

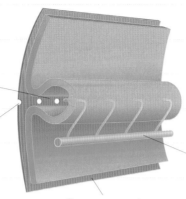

Cavity of lateral line canal

Pores in the scales allow water to enter the lateral line canal.

Outer layer of scales

◀ *The line of pores running from head to tail along the flanks of a fish are the openings to the lateral line, a sensory organ system that responds to pressure waves and gives fish awareness of nearby objects.*

Nerve fiber carrying impulses to the spinal cord and then to the brain.

SINGLES, PAIRS OR GROUPS?

Some fish should be kept as single specimens, either because they fight with each other at the least provocation or because they require a territory and there is insufficient space for more than one. Where fish can be sexed, it is wise to buy a pair; but if they cannot be easily sexed, then the minimum number may be just two. You should keep shoaling fish in a shoal, not only because they look good but also because this is how they live in the wild.

▼ *The female ram (Microgeophagus ramirezi) is smaller than the male (bottom).*

▲ *Like all tetras, red phantom tetras (Megalamphodus sweglesi) are shoaling fish that will not thrive if kept singly.*

LIGHT AND DARK

Fish enter a sleeplike state at night, which is vital to their health. Aim to have the aquarium light on for 10–12 hours a day, and make sure there is some light in the room when the tank light switches on and off to avoid sharp, sudden changes in light levels. Use an automatic timer to achieve a regular day/night cycle.

Communities of fish

Beginners to the fish-keeping hobby tend to choose a bit of everything with which to stock their first aquarium. This first collection of fish is generally described as a community, and if chosen with care, such community fish will tolerate similar conditions and have either a peaceful disposition or will have a healthy disregard of each other. However, this term is only a guide, as not all community fish will coexist without causing problems. For example, a fish that is likely to nip at long-finned species may still be considered a community fish because it will live perfectly happily in a community of fish without long fins. Some quieter-natured fish prefer to be kept in a peaceful environment and may become stressed if kept with overactive species, yet both may still be described as community fish. Always check the individual needs of the fish you intend to house together.

AQUARIUM ZONES

A HELPING HAND

Many fish have attributes that can be put to good use in the aquarium. Scavengers will rummage around, dislodging particles that can then be removed by the filter, whereas other fish may eat algae or dead plant leaves. Including fish such as these will help to keep your aquarium clean.

Fish swimming at all levels make an attractive and well-balanced community aquarium.

TOP

Many top-dwelling fish take food from the surface: in the wild, insects, fruits, and seeds float on the water. Some are good jumpers and the tank will need a tightly fitting cover.

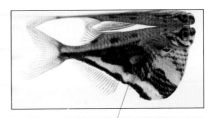

The hatchetfish is a surface dweller.

MIDDLE

The middle area can be home to active shoaling fish that make use of the open areas, such as tetras, and also to more sedate, slow-moving species, such as angelfish and gouramis.

Scissortail rasboras prefer the middle area of the tank.

BOTTOM

Bottom-dwelling fish are another characteristic group; many are nocturnal by nature, hiding away among plants and rocks by day. These include many catfish and loaches.

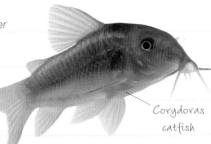

Corydoras catfish

COMPATIBILITY

Compatibility

Many new fish keepers are surprised to discover that their fish have very individual characteristics and behave very differently from one another. In the confines of the aquarium, the conflicts that occur between fish with different social rules can be distressing to the fish and an unwelcome disruption to the aquarium community. Considering which species will get along with one another is important when choosing and buying your fish, and understanding why some fish might conflict will help you achieve a peaceful mix.

WHAT MAKES A COMMUNITY FISH?

The term *community fish*, which is applied to any species that is not by nature overly aggressive or territorial, does not necessarily mean it will get along with all other fish. Rather, a community fish is simply a fish that can be kept without problems in a community of compatible species. To work out which species are compatible with a particular community fish, you will need to find out a few details about the species' characteristics. The most important of these are size, preferred numbers, spawning nature, activity level, ratio of males to females, and territorial tendencies.

▲ *In a well-thought-out aquarium, the fish will live together in harmony.*

SIZE

Although only a small proportion of fish are exclusively predators, most fish will take the opportunity to eat small fish if they are easy to catch and in close proximity. Some fish will take this opportunity, if available, at night, when the victim is in a state of low awareness. In addition to the chances of predation, smaller fish will become stressed by the presence of much larger individuals and may be outcompeted for food. Always check the eventual size of any fish you intend to purchase, and avoid fish that are twice as big as your smallest fish.

The jaguar catfish will prey on smaller fish.

NUMBERS

Some fish are shoaling species, whereas others prefer to be on their own. If the number requirements of a fish are ignored, their normal behavior can change, and they will become unpredictable. Shoaling fish kept in small numbers can become timid, reclusive, and unhealthy, or they can become aggressive, nippy, and troublesome. Fish that are natural loners may either ignore others of the same type or become territorial, with the dominant fish continually bullying the weaker ones. If a fish is a shoaling species, it must be kept in a group, normally of at least six or more. If it is a loner, keep only one of that species unless further research reveals that you can keep several. It is also best to avoid keeping very closely related species together.

▲ *The well-known red-tailed black shark* (Epalzeorhynchos bicolor) *is best kept singly. Small numbers will result in one individual becoming a dominant bully.*

▼ *A male cichlid* Aequidens rivulatus *is mouthing a female to stimulate breeding. Such fish aggressively defend their eggs.*

SPAWNING NATURE

A fish's behavior can change dramatically if a pair decides to spawn. This is most often the case with members of the cichlid family, which are generally very good parents and will aggressively defend spawning sites, eggs, and young fry. Always check to see if your fish are likely to spawn in the future. If they are defensive parents, allow plenty of space in the aquarium, and mix them only with robust fish that will be able to handle any changes in their tankmates' behavior.

Compatibility (continued)

Fish may be slow moving, with a quiet demeanor, or fast moving and boisterous. Often, their behavior is related to the conditions prevailing in their natural habitats. Bear in mind that in the confines of the aquarium, slow fish will be disturbed by boisterous species and may lose out at feeding times or be damaged by knocks from other fish. In instances like this, the slower fish may become stressed and ill, reclusive, or stunted from a lack of sufficient food. Active fish that grow only to around 2–2.75 in. (5–7 cm) can normally be mixed with any fish, since they are too small to cause harm, but larger active fish should be kept only with similar-natured species.

▲ *Fish of a similar disposition are likely to be good tankmates.*

MALE TO FEMALE RATIO

Male fish of many species, even those considered peaceful community varieties, will attempt to become dominant within their species type or group. This happens because a dominant male is more likely to secure good spawning grounds and pass on strong genes to its offspring, so it will be more attractive to females. In addition, some males will continually harass females in an attempt to mate. Check to see if any fish you purchase has such tendencies, and try to obtain a suitable mix of males and females. To avoid harassment, chose only one sex or choose two females to every male. To avoid problems of dominance, choose only one male and several females or a group of more than four males, so that it is difficult for one to become dominant.

▼ *Keeping a single male swordtail (left) with two or three females will protect the females from harassment.*

ROGUE FISH

Although the behavior of most fish can be predicted from general experience and accepted observations, it is not uncommon to have a rogue fish that behaves differently. In these cases, the fish's behavior can often be toned down by the addition of specially selected fish that are large and robust enough to be a threat, yet peaceful enough not to endanger other fish. Many peaceful barb or rainbow fish species can be used for this purpose, and once added to the tank, the rogue fish often calms down. As long as there are no other conflicts, it sometimes helps simply to increase the numbers of the species of which one is a rogue. The rogue fish will then have too many fish of the same type to conflict with and will reduce its antisocial behavior accordingly.

◀ *Adding a peaceful species, such as this Lake Tebera rainbow fish (Melanotaenia herbertaxelrodi), may help calm down a rogue fish.*

KEEPING LISTS

If you buy your fish from a good retailer, there will be knowledgeable staff on hand who can advise you on which fish can be safely kept together. If you keep a list of all the species in your aquarium, it will make the retailer's job of recommending suitable species much easier. Such a list will also give you grounds for returning a fish if it becomes troublesome, even though your retailer advised that it was suitable for your community.

TERRITORIAL NATURE

Some fish are naturally territorial and aggressive; the worst offenders should not be labeled as general community fish, although with correct tankmates, they can be kept in a specific community of fish. If you are looking to add any fish that are naturally aggressive, it would be wise to do as much research as possible and choose their tankmates with great care.

▶ *Male dwarf gouramis are generally peaceful, although some individuals can be disruptive—either aggressive or sulky.*

WATER QUALITY

Water quality

In a community collection, it is impossible to give each species the exact water conditions that it enjoyed in nature, but you should familiarize yourself with some basic water chemistry in order to understand the needs of the fish. Depending on where you live, your tap water will have varying degrees of minerals present, which makes it either acid, neutral, or alkaline and hard or soft. A fish shop near you will acclimatize the fish you buy to the local water conditions so you can keep them in your aquarium. However, some fish can be kept only under certain conditions, and these may be labeled as soft water or hard water species. To keep these more specialized fish, you may need to seek additional advice from your shop.

PH LEVELS

The pH value is an indication of whether water is acidic, neutral, or alkaline. The scale extends from 0 to 14, with 0 being extremely acidic and 14 extremely alkaline. pH 7 represents the neutral point. The pH scale is logarithmic, with each unit reflecting a tenfold difference. Therefore, pH 6 is ten times more acidic than pH 7 and 100 times more acidic than pH 8.

WATER HARDNESS

Water hardness is a measure of the dissolved salts it carries, mainly carbonates and sulphates of calcium and magnesium. Water with a high salt content is referred to as hard, whereas water low in these salts is referred to as soft. In most natural environments, the pH value and hardness are linked, with low pH water being soft and high pH water being hard.

Discus live in the Amazon River.

Electric blue hap
(*Scianochromis ahli*) from Lake Malawi

▲ The natural environments of aquarium fish can differ markedly in the pH value of their native waters. For example, Lake Malawi cichlids (above) live in hard, highly alkaline waters (pH 8–8.5), whereas discus (above right) come from areas with soft, acidic water (pH 6). Not surprisingly, you will never find these two types of fish thriving in the same aquarium.

* Tap water is processed to make it fit for human consumption. The chemicals added by the water company make it safe for us to drink, but dangerous for aquarium fish. Treat it with a tap water conditioner before use.

KEEPING WATER CLEAN

Fish excrete waste in the aquarium, which results in the production of ammonia and nitrites, both toxic to fish. A filter will remove ammonia and nitrite by creating a suitable home for bacteria to grow and feed on the toxins, but this can take a little time. The bacteria that settle in the filter only grow as waste levels in the aquarium increase. This is why you must allow waste levels to build up slowly and steadily, which can be achieved by stocking the tank with fish slowly and taking care not to overfeed the fish.

Always use the same brand of test kit to be sure of obtaining consistent results.

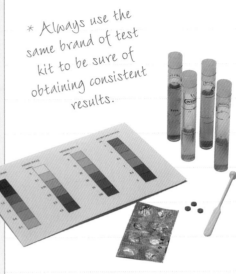

▲ The only way to monitor levels of ammonia and nitrite is to test the tank water regularly. In a new tank, test for ammonia and nitrite at least twice a week for the first few weeks. Reduce the feeding if either of these pollutants is present.

WATER TEMPERATURE

Temperature fluctuations in the water can be very damaging to life in the aquarium. Most tropical fish can be kept at a temperature of 75–80°F (24–26°C), but always check the requirements of the fish you buy. When carrying out water changes, make sure that the new water is within a few degrees of the aquarium water, or introduce it slowly over a period of time. In addition to shocking the fish, changes in temperature can kill filter bacteria, resulting in increased pollution levels.

Oxygen levels are reduced at higher temperatures. During the summer, fish may appreciate extra aeration in the aquarium.

▲ Golden and green sailfin mollies (Poecilia velifera) and black mollies (P. sphenops) come from both fresh and brackish environments, although most tank-bred specimens will benefit from brackish water. Add a little aquarium salt to the tank to help them retain good health and color.

Aquascaping

To help you plan your aquarium, it is a good idea to prepare simple overhead and front-view sketches of the proposed display. Consider the needs of the fish at this stage: would they appreciate the odd cave, a dense planting area, floating plants, or hiding places? If you would like to encourage the fish to breed, think about materials that will create suitable breeding sites. Anabantoids, such as gouramis, will require a number of small floating plants, fine-leaved species such as *Cabomba,* and a calm surface on which to build a bubblenest. Dwarf cichlids, such as kribs, appreciate caves or small flat rocks and well-defined territorial areas.

▲ It is worth making a sketch of your aquarium display before you start aquascaping. Remember to consider the needs of the fish, as well as the overall design and appearance.

◄ In nature, the substrate is rarely uniform and flat. It is likely to be undulating and littered with bits of stone, wood, and organic debris. In the aquarium, scattering rock chips, pebbles, and broken wood, over the main substrate looks more natural.

ROCKS IN THE AQUARIUM

Your choice of rocks should reflect the style of aquarium you are creating and suit the fish you plan to keep. For example, large, jagged pieces of slate are ideal for a mountain stream display housing fish that enjoy fast-flowing water, such as zebra danios and White Cloud Mountain minnows. If you are setting up a tank for Malawi cichlids, choose smooth rounded boulders or cobbles. If you prefer a lighter material, lava rock and tufa are easy to stack together to create rockscapes.

▲ Lava rock is very light and ideal for constructing rockscapes. Select suitable pieces and glue them together with aquarium sealant.

PLACING DECOR

To create a varied environment for the fish, make sure there are plenty of hiding places and areas of cover and also sufficient open areas for swimming. Decor and/or dense planting around the edges and rear of the display aquarium not only provide hiding spots but also conceal equipment, while leaving a central open area for swimming.

▲ *Pieces of bogwood add structure and create divisions between planting areas.*

◀ *Surface plants, such as* Salvinia natans, *provide welcome shade and cover for the fish.*

MIX AND MATCH PLANTS

Individual plant species all have a place in the aquarium. Species with tall stems or large leaves work well as background plants, whereas smaller plants suit the midground, and low-growing species are best in the foreground. However, there are no set rules for what constitutes a foreground or background plant, and it is often better to mix up the areas a little. Rather than use many different species, it may be more effective to use a limited number of species in larger groupings.

▲ *Pellia* (Monosolenium tenerum), *a small-leaved, fernlike plant, is sold attached to rocks or stones. Fish enjoy rummaging in the foliage of this foreground plant.*

▲ C. walkeri *is a commonly available midground plant. It often looks best once it has spread, creating a dense group. Here it contrasts well with the bamboo.*

◀ *Larger species of* Echinodorus *are ideal for the background of spacious displays. Given a nutrient-rich substrate, iron fertilization and bright lighting, the plants are easy to care for.*

AQUASCAPING

An aquarium setup

To demonstrate setting up an aquarium, we have chosen a standard-size tank measuring 24 x 12 x 15 in. (60 x 30 x 38 cm) high. Although relatively small, this aquarium holds enough water to prevent any rapid fluctuations in water conditions, such as temperature and pH, that would stress the fish. Generally speaking, buying the largest aquarium you can afford and accommodate is a good investment. Besides enabling you to keep more fish, the more water it holds, the more stable the environment will be.

CHOOSING A GOOD LOCATION

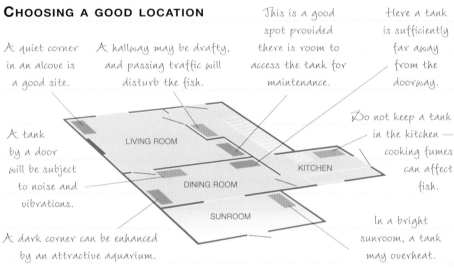

A quiet corner in an alcove is a good site.

A hallway may be drafty, and passing traffic will disturb the fish.

This is a good spot provided there is room to access the tank for maintenance.

Here a tank is sufficiently far away from the doorway.

A tank by a door will be subject to noise and vibrations.

Do not keep a tank in the kitchen — cooking fumes can affect fish.

A dark corner can be enhanced by an attractive aquarium.

In a bright sunroom, a tank may overheat.

THE TANK AND STAND

The hood is part of this self-assembly unit and houses a condensation tray and a shelf for the light.

◀ Tanks must sit on a strong cabinet or stand — an existing piece of furniture may not be able to support a tank full of water.

Set a glass tank on a layer of polystyrene to even out any imperfections in the baseboard or cabinet.

Cupboards can house external filters and cables.

Position the stand so that the weight of the water is taken by the joists, not the floorboards.

WHAT TO LOOK FOR

There is a great difference between systemized tanks with built-in filtration, heating, and lighting and tanks sold as package deals with ancillary equipment stacked inside. If the extras are what you would choose to buy anyway, these collections represent good value; if not, it is best to buy a plain tank and add the accessories separately.

Secondhand tanks are inexpensive but carry many risks. Often they come with equipment and fish you do not want, and there is no warranty if they leak or if the equipment fails.

▶ *Clean the tank with a lint-free cloth and water. Never use detergents, which can be lethal to fish.*

CHECKING THE LEVEL

Even a slight discrepancy in the level will be obvious once you add water to the aquarium.

▲ *Make sure that both the tank and stand are level in all directions by placing a long spirit level along all the edges. If necessary, rest the spirit level on a straight wooden bar. Always adjust the cabinet or stand, not the tank.*

▲ *Choose a background that suits the style of your tank. Often, a plain blue or black background is the most effective.*

▲ *Fitting a suitable background to the external back of the glass serves two purposes: it can create the illusion of extra depth and hide the wallpaper behind it. Fit the background before you move the tank into its final position and fill it with water.*

An aquarium setup (continued)

Natural sand and gravel are available in various grades. The best types have rounded grains and are lime free. Some fish like to bury in the substrate, and others feed by sifting through it. In this case, river sand or fine or medium gravel is suitable. Coarse gravel can be used with larger fish species, but debris and uneaten food can become trapped in the gaps between the grains. Mix different substrates for a more natural effect.

HEATER SIZE

As a guide, allow 50 watts per 7 gallons (27 L) of water. For larger tanks, consider splitting the total wattage between two smaller heaters. This provides more even heating and prevents a rapid temperature change if one heater fails.

Submersible pump provides the power source

Foam cartridge houses beneficial bacteria

Plastic barrel with internal divider for good water flow

◀ *Internal power filters are suitable for smaller tanks. Filters work by taking in dirty water, passing it through the filter medium, and returning it to the aquarium. Never run the filter pump without water in the tank.*

Place the Heaterstat at an angle, slightly above the substrate.

Position the filter with the nozzle facing outward.

Do not cover units with substrate, as they will overheat.

The filter is held in a cradle.

Leave a gap for water to circulate.

◀ *Before use, wash gravel well. Clean it in batches until the water drains clear.*

River sand

Fine gravel

Medium gravel

Coarse gravel

▲ Buy your wood and rocks only from aquatic dealers. Unsuitable rock types contain dangerous metals or substances that alter water chemistry, and some woods can rot and pollute the aquarium.

▼ Using a jug, pour the water gently onto a flat surface. As the water level rises, you can use a bucket. Do not fill the tank to the top, as it will overflow when you add the plants. Switch on the power supply.

CONDITIONING WATER

Using a tap-water conditioner makes the water safe for fish. Follow the manufacturer's directions.

You can position wood in front of the heater, but make sure it does not rest against it.

Add heavy rocks with care, and bed them into the substrate until they rest on the glass.

◀ Scrub bogwood and soak it for several days to reduce the tannins that stain the water.

◀ Brush and wash rocks to remove dust and plant matter that could foul the water.

An aquarium setup (continued)

Leave the tank for 24 hours or so before adding the plants, by which time the filtration system should have removed any cloudiness in the water. Select plants by size, leaf shape, and color, using tall ones for the back of the aquarium and medium and short ones for the center and front. Put in each plant individually, and allow enough space between them for light to reach the substrate. Plant in staggered rows so that the whole grouping looks like a wall of plants from the front. Leave swimming space for the fish. Switch off all electrical equipment before starting work on the aquarium.

◀ Remove the metal strip from the base of the cabombas, and separate each cutting.

◀ Using sharp scissors, cut away the damaged stem just below a leaf joint

▶ Hold the vallisneria near the base. Using a finger of the same hand, make a hole in the gravel, and slide the plant gently into the substrate.

Start planting at the rear of the tank and work toward the front. Space the plants so that their leaves are just touching.

The feathery cabomba softens the edges of the wood.

Vallisneria leaves conceal the filter and sway in the gentle water flow.

Continue to plant the tank. Ludwigia and bacopa could fill this gap.

▶ Remove the Amazon sword from its basket, and tease away the medium around the base.

◀ Plant each small cryptocoryne individually to give it sufficient space to grow and spread.

THE HOOD

The hood houses the light source that promotes healthy plant growth and allows you to see your fish. There are different styles of hood, so before assembling it, make sure you understand the steps involved and have everything at hand.

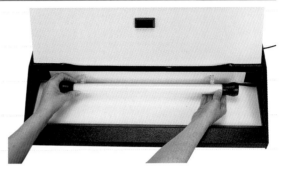

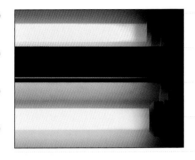

▲ *Place the starter unit into the back chamber of the hood. Connect the tube to the end caps, and push it onto the clips.*

◀ *For a balanced light output, choose a fluorescent tube with the three required peaks of blue, red, and yellow. These are best produced by a triphosphor tube. A pink tube will enhance plant growth.*

Control the lighting with a timer, and keep it running for up to 12–14 hours a day.

Choose a hood with good access for feeding.

Check heaters, filters, and other equipment every day to ensure that they are operating correctly.

Check the reading every day.

Prune plants regularly and replant cuttings.

The completed aquarium will take at least five weeks to mature. A filter start-up product helps to speed up the process.

Take time to enjoy your aquarium, and change your viewpoint slightly every day.

Choosing and adding fish

Surface area determines how many fish you can keep in an aquarium. For freshwater species you need 30 in^2. (75 cm^2) of surface area per 1 in. (2.5 cm) body length of fish. A tank measuring 24 x 12 in. (60 x 30 cm) has a surface area of 74 in^2. (188 cm^2) and will hold about 24 in^2. (60 cm^2) of freshwater tropical fish. Allow for growth when choosing fish.

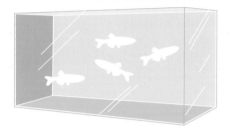

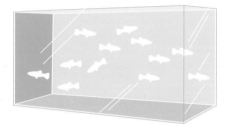

▲ This 24 x 12 in. (60 x 30 cm) tank has four fish, each 6 in. (15 cm) long, which together add up to the maximum carrying capacity of 24 in. (60 cm) of fish body length.

▲ This 24 x 12 in. (60 x 30 cm) tank has 12 fish, each 2 in. (5 cm) long, the maximum carrying capacity of 24 in. (60 cm) of fish body length.

◀ Always seek the advice of a good dealer. Make a list of all the fish you like, then work out which will mix together and which will cause problems until you have a suitable selection. This avoids the disappointment of discovering that a fish you want to add later on is unsuitable for keeping with the stock you already have.

WHAT TO LOOK FOR

All sales tanks should be clean and clearly labeled with details on the fish on sale, including price and potential size. Some dealers also give feeding information and details of other special requirements, plus compatibility advice. Never buy apparently healthy fish from a tank containing dead or sick specimens.

CHOOSE HEALTHY FISH

Check that fish are active and behaving normally. Shoaling fish should be swimming with their fins held out, whereas bottom-dwelling species will be grubbing on the substrate searching for food. Avoid buying fish with split fins, badly damaged barbels, pinched-looking bellies, or sunken eyes.

* Do not be surprised if you see tanks in quarantine at your local store or notices that say something like "New arrivals, not on sale yet." This is your retailer looking after his stock and a sign of a good store.

◀ *The dealer places the fish in a plastic bag with some water and a great deal of air. Placing the fish in a dark outer wrapping makes their journey home less stressful.*

▲ *After a short journey, float the unopened bag in the aquarium for about 20 minutes to equalize the temperatures.*

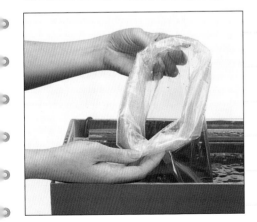

▲ *After a long journey—say more than 30 minutes—first roll down the sides of the bag to give the fish some fresh air.*

▲ *Release the fish gently into the tank, turning the bag on its side and encouraging the fish to swim out.*

CHOOSING AND ADDING FISH

FEEDING FISH

Feeding fish

With such a wide range of foods available, feeding fish a healthy, balanced diet is not difficult. Take into account the feeding habits of your fish (do they feed at the surface or at the bottom of the tank?) and their size. If your tank contains fish of widely differing sizes, tailor the particle size of stick or pellet food to the mouths of the smallest, not the largest, inhabitants. Large-particle food is unlikely to soften in time for the small fish to get their share. Stick foods can be easily snapped into manageable portions, whereas pellets are available in all grades from fine to coarse.

DRIED FOODS

Additives in food can enhance the colors of tropical fish.

Flake foods can provide the staple diet for most fish. Offer them sparingly.

Stick foods are useful for feeding the larger barbs.

Pellets are available in floating or sinking types for all tank regions.

FROZEN FOODS

Gamma-irradiated frozen foods are often sold in variety blister packs, containing, for example, bloodworm, daphnia, and glassworms. Buy one of these first and note which varieties your fish prefer. Then you can buy the favored foods in single-variety blister packs.

Thaw out cubes of frozen food before offering them to the fish.

FEEDING STRATEGIES

Feeding your fish once a day is fine. A hungry (but not starving) fish is a healthy fish. With dried and frozen foods, feed only what the fish will consume in a couple of minutes, and make sure they eat it all so that it does not pollute the aquarium. Green foods can be left until the next feed for herbivorous fish to browse on. Fish benefit from a varied diet; provide dried, live, and frozen foods.

◀ Fish will relish offerings of live foods, such as bloodworm, daphnia, and brine shrimp. Earthworms dug from a chemical-free garden or collected from lawns are equally irresistible. Redworms from angling shops are a good alternative.

SUITABLE GREEN FOODS

▶ Herbivorous fish such as plecs appreciate fresh greens. Suitable items include blanched lettuce leaves, fresh garden peas (pinched to remove the skins), and raw zucchini or cucumber slices. Nontoxic lettuce clips are available from aquatic shops. Remove uneaten food before it starts to rot.

Blanched lettuce leaves

Cucumber and zucchini

Fresh peas

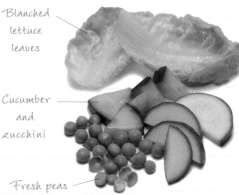

◀ These zebra danios swim at all levels in the aquarium. When feeding flake food to a community of fish made up of surface, midwater, and bottom feeders, hold a pinch under the water for a few seconds before releasing it. Some of the flakes will then sink, making it more likely that all the fish get their fair share.

If all the food is left to float, surface-feeders will monopolize the meal at the expense of other fish.

▲ The upturned mouth makes it easy for mollies to take food from the surface.

BROAD TASTES

Although some tropical fish are classed as herbivores and others as carnivores, all but out-and-out predators have a mixed diet in the wild. Algae-eating bristlenose plecs, for example, also eat the tiny creatures found amid the greenery, and livebearers take insect food as well as soft plant matter.

FEEDING FISH

Aquarium maintenance

Regular maintenance is essential to keep your fish and plants healthy and your tank looking its best. Most tasks take only a few minutes and should be seen as a pleasure, not a chore. It is impossible to lay down a set schedule, as tank needs vary according to the number and species of fish they contain and the type of filtration used. Start by working out a maintenance timetable of daily, weekly or biweekly, monthly, and occasional jobs. With the help of an aquarium log, you will soon be able to adapt these to your setup. If anything goes wrong, you may need to rethink only what needs attending to and when.

ESSENTIAL TASKS

Daily
- Remove uneaten food
- Check the health of the fish
- Check the water temperature
- Check that filters, lights, air pumps, etc. are working properly

Weekly/every two weeks
- Make a 20–25% partial water change
- Test water for pH, ammonia, nitrite, and nitrate levels
- Remove dead plant matter; vacuum substrate with a gravel cleaner

- Clean algae from the front glass
- Clean cover glass/condensation tray

Monthly/as required
- Clean filter and replace expendable media if required

Every 6-12 months
- Service air pump and filter/power head motors
- Replace lighting tubes
- Replace airstones and airline
- Scrub rocks/bogwood and plastic plants to remove built-up algae

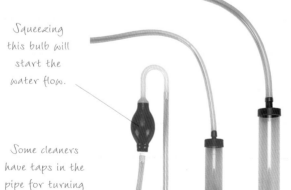

Squeezing this bulb will start the water flow.

Some cleaners have taps in the pipe for turning the siphon on and off.

◀ Various gravel cleaners are available, although all work on the same basic principle of gravitational suction, removing lighter wastes while leaving the substrate relatively intact.

Different-size gravel cleaners are available for different tank sizes.

◀ *Water test kits are easy to use, following the manufacturer's directions. This nitrite test has produced no color, which indicates a safe zero nitrite level. During the first week or two of a new aquarium you can expect to experience slight nitrite readings. If you continue to read nitrite levels above 0.1 mg/L after this period, you may be overfeeding or overstocking, or the filter may not be performing correctly.*

CLEANING AN EXTERNAL FILTER

1 Turn the coupling taps to the off position, and undo the plastic nuts securing the taps to the filter body. Place the filter in a bowl and tilt it to drain off most of the water inside.

2 Remove the motor from the canister. Take the impeller from its housing, and clean it of slime and debris, wiping down all the plastic parts with a damp cloth. Remove the internal slotted basket.

3 Remove the media from the internal basket. Discard the soiled filter floss and exhausted activated carbon (if used). Gently wash the foam pads or ceramic pieces. Replace the carbon and then the filter floss. Reassemble the unit, couple the filter to the taps, and turn them on. Water should siphon down into the canister. If not, prime as instructed.

◀ *Using an algae magnet, you can easily clean the inside of the tank.*

◀ *Trim tall or bushy plants as needed, and replenish fertilizers.*

BREEDING

Breeding

In most aquariums, the fish will be breeding off and on just about all the time. The trick is to stop the other fish from eating any eggs or young. Fish use a wide range of breeding strategies, some of which are highly specialized. Most aquarium fish can be described as egg scatterers or egg depositors, bubblenesters, or livebearers. Cichlids practice parental care and have specific needs in the aquarium. To breed most fish successfully, it is best to set up a separate spawning/fry-rearing tank.

BREEDING SETUP FOR EGG SCATTERERS

The cherry barb *(Puntius titteya)*, like many other barbs, tetras, and minnows, is an egg scatterer. Condition the adults for a couple of weeks, and then place a plump female with a brightly colored male into the breeding tank, preferably late in the evening. Spawning may take several hours, and the eggs are left hanging among plant fronds. Remove the parents to give the eggs a chance of surviving until they hatch a day later. Feed them on liquid fry food for a week, then newly hatched brine shrimp, microworms, and powdered fry food. Keep a lookout for signs of velvet disease as the fry grow up.

Have plenty of bunches of fine-leaved plants or artificial spawning mops.

Use clean, slightly acidic water. Allow it to stand for a few days before adding the fish.

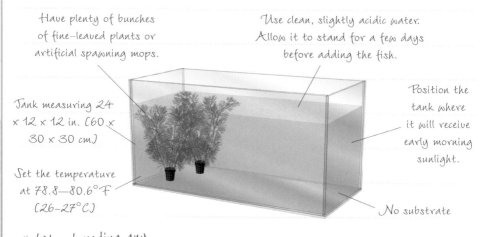

Tank measuring 24 x 12 x 12 in. [60 x 30 x 30 cm]

Set the temperature at 78.8—80.6°F [26–27°C]

Position the tank where it will receive early morning sunlight.

No substrate

* When breeding any fish, select only those with strong, robust bodies and perfectly formed fins. Avoid fish with deformities such as a crooked spine, which could be a genetic fault.

◀ As immature fish, both male and female cherry barbs are a very similar pale pink color. As they mature, males develop a bright scarlet color.

BREEDING SETUP FOR EGG DEPOSITORS

To spawn the egg-depositing harlequin rasbora *(Trigonostigma heteromorpha)*, place a well-conditioned adult male with a younger plump female in the aquarium late in the evening. As the pair spawn, they turn upside down and deposit their eggs in batches underneath a suitable leaf. Although the parents are not rabid egg eaters, remove them as soon as possible afterward. The eggs hatch the following day, and the fry are free-swimming on the third day. Give them infusoria or liquid fry foods for a week, then brine shrimp. They grow rapidly.

Tank measuring 24 x 12 x 12 in. (60 x 30 x 30 cm)

Use very soft and moderately acidic water.

Set up a thickly planted area with broad-leaved plants, such as cryptocoryne.

Add a few clumps of fine-leaved plants, such as cabomba.

Sand or fine gravel substrate

BREEDING SETUP FOR BUBBLENESTERS

The male Siamese fighting fish constructs a bubblenest at the surface, anchored to the tank sides or underneath a polystyrene tile or cup. Remove the female after spawning. The male collects the eggs, places them in the nest, and guards them until they are free-swimming. Remove the male at this point. Feed the young on infusoria at first.

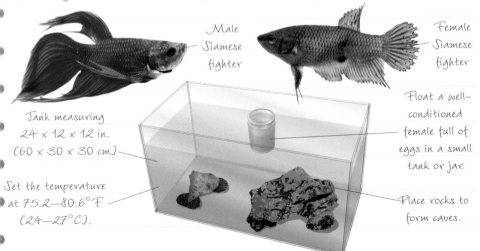

Male Siamese fighter

Female Siamese fighter

Tank measuring 24 x 12 x 12 in. (60 x 30 x 30 cm)

Float a well-conditioned female full of eggs in a small tank or jar.

Set the temperature at 75.2–80.6°F (24–27°C).

Place rocks to form caves.

BREEDING

Breeding (continued)

The cultivated forms of platy, molly, guppy, and swordtail available in the trade are prolific, but because they are all of hybrid origin, maintaining or creating a good-quality strain presents difficulties. However, just saving a few young and rearing them is not a problem. In mature males, the anal fin is modified to form a rodlike structure called a gonopodium, which is used to transfer sperm to the female. When the female shows signs of being pregnant, move her to the rearing tank until the fry are born; then remove her. Gestation is about 28 days, and the female gives birth to fully formed live young.

BREEDING SETUP FOR LIVEBEARERS

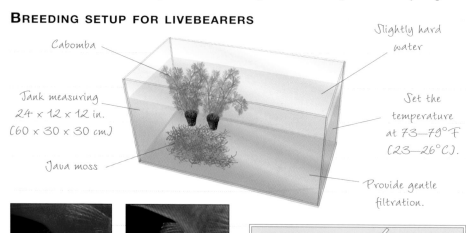

Cabomba

Slightly hard water

Tank measuring 24 × 12 × 12 in. (60 × 30 × 30 cm)

Set the temperature at 73–79°F (23–26°C).

Java moss

Provide gentle filtration.

▲ In the male platy (right), the anal fin has become an internal organ of fertilization called the gonopodium.

* If you are serious about breeding your fish, find out as much as you can about their individual requirements and those of the fry. Some fish need water parameters similar to those found in their natural habitat. Some fry will require live food cultures.

▲ To make a V-trap for livebearing fish, seal two pieces of glass vertically to opposite sides of the breeding tank, leaving a small gap wide enough for the fry to swim through but not the parents. Add some plants on the side that will receive the fry, and place the parents in the empty area. Livebearers that swim to the surface at birth circle around the edges looking for cover, find the gap, and swim through to the plants on the other side.

MAKING A BREEDING TRAP

The idea of a breeding trap is that eggs or newborn fry drop through the openings and are safe from predation by their parents or other fish. You can make your own using plastic-coated wire mesh that is large enough to allow eggs or fry through but not the adults. Form it into a basket a little smaller than the breeding tank, and suspend it in the tank by two pieces of wire. The top of the basket should protrude 1 in. (2.5 cm) or more above the water surface. The trap and the parent fish can be removed after spawning, leaving the eggs or fry to develop undisturbed.

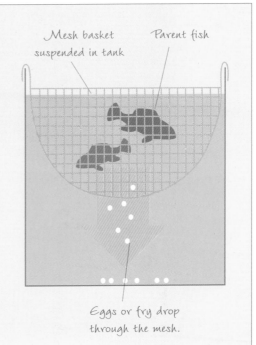

Mesh basket suspended in tank

Parent fish

Eggs or fry drop through the mesh.

BREEDING SETUP FOR KRIBS

The krib *(Pelvicachromis pulcher)* is a typical cave-spawning cichlid. The female of a settled pair will select a suitable spawning cave and entice her mate into it. They usually spawn on the roof, and the eggs take three days to hatch, becoming free-swimming on the seventh day. Feed the fry on brine shrimp and microworms at first. Adults will rear their brood without any problems for months. Remove the young when their parents drive them away from the old nesting site and prepare to spawn again.

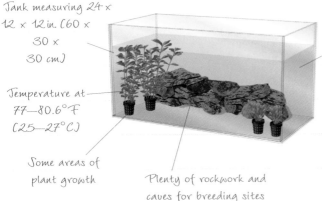

Tank measuring 24 x 12 x 12 in. (60 x 30 x 30 cm)

Temperature at 77–80.6°F (25–27°C)

Some areas of plant growth

Plenty of rockwork and caves for breeding sites

Moderately soft, neutral water

▼ Female kribs have a deeper body than males.

Health care

Under normal conditions, the fish's immune systems prevent diseases taking hold, but problems occur when a fish becomes stressed or is physically injured, or when the background levels of harmful disease organisms rise dangerously. Taking care not to overstock the tank, quarantining new fish, monitoring water conditions, and keeping the aquarium clean will prevent the outbreak of most diseases.

QUARANTINING FISH

When buying your second and subsequent fish, even from a reliable dealer, it is always safest to quarantine them in a separate tank before adding them to the main display aquarium. If they do need any medication, treatment will be easier in the quarantine tank, and it can also allow them to rest and acclimatize to your water conditions. Ideally, keep them isolated for four weeks, but certainly no less than one.

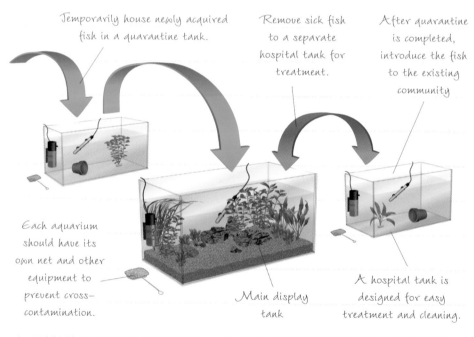

Temporarily house newly acquired fish in a quarantine tank.

Remove sick fish to a separate hospital tank for treatment.

After quarantine is completed, introduce the fish to the existing community

Each aquarium should have its own net and other equipment to prevent cross-contamination.

Main display tank

A hospital tank is designed for easy treatment and cleaning.

▲ Equip a quarantine tank with a simple internal sponge filter, a Heaterstat, some decor, and a shallow layer of gravel. Check water quality regularly. The pH level should match that of the main aquarium, unless a fish has come from a retailer with different water. In this case, gradually alter the pH level until it is the same as that in the display aquarium. Do not subject fish to a daily change in pH of more than 0.3 of a unit. Maintain ammonia and nitrite levels at zero, with nitrate below 25 ppm.

OTHER USES

If a fish becomes sick or distressed, transfer it to the quarantine tank, which then becomes a hospital tank. You can also use the quarantine tank to temporarily house a fish that is being harassed or bullied. If any fry are produced in the main aquarium, remove them to the quarantine tank until they are large enough to be housed with the other fish.

▼ *Eyes can tell you a lot. Cloudy eyes (below) indicate that a fish is unhappy with its water quality, while sunken eyes show that the fish is seriously ill. A single bulging eye can be the result of violence from a tankmate, or infection, perhaps from poor conditions. Bulging eyes are also one of the symptoms of dropsy. A single blind eye is probably a deformity.*

WHITE SPOT LIFE CYCLE

Understanding the life cycle can help you apply effective treatment.

Parasites break through the skin and become free-swimming. Bacteria may affect the exit wound.

Free-swimming parasites break out of the cyst and must find a fish host within 24 hours.

Break the cycle here using a proprietary treatment to eliminate free-swimming parasites.

Inside the cyst, cells multiply rapidly.

Within hours, each parasite forms a cyst around itself.

▲ *White spot is highly contagious. Chemical treatments are aimed at the free-swimming stage of the parasite's life cycle and are very effective. Although the cysts quickly disappear from the host fish, the treatment must be allowed to affect the free-swimming parasites.*

* *When using medications, always follow the maker's directions and never use two treatments at the same time.*

Health care (continued)

Sometimes, the symptoms of several diseases can resemble one another. As a (very general) guide to help you make a diagnosis, bacterial diseases develop the fastest: in severe cases, from first signs to death in around 24 hours. Next are fungal infections, which almost always manifest as fluffy blobs (see below). Parasitic illnesses are generally slower, developing and spreading among individuals over a period of days.

HEALTH CARE

BACTERIAL INFECTIONS

Symptoms include fin rot, mouth rot, ulcers, pop eye, bloodshot areas, and swelling or emaciation of the abdomen. Treat superficial infections with over-the-counter remedies; more severe ones require prescription antibiotics. Try also to establish the original cause: could something have lowered your fish's resistance?

Pinecone scales may be caused by a bacterial infection.

FUNGAL INFECTIONS

Fungal spores are constantly present in aquatic environments. Healthy fish can resist them, but they will invade damaged tissues or even intact ones if the overall immune system is severely suppressed. If a fish is stressed, has a wound, or has another infection, it may well also pick up a fungus. Fungus appears as whitish, fluffy blobs resembling cotton wool, and needs to be treated immediately with over-the-counter remedies.

A BULLYING PROBLEM?

The symptoms of bullying or sexual harassment can mimic those of some diseases: clamped or ragged fins (below), battered or slimy-looking flanks, hiding, and refusing to eat. Transfer affected fish to a quarantine tank. If it looks better with no other treatment, you probably do have a bullying problem.

PARASITIC ILLNESSES

Look for slimy or cloudy skin, clamped fins, and rapid or heavy breathing, particularly in livebearers. Sometimes there are pale patches on the body. If an over-the-counter parasite remedy does not seem to work, contact your veterinarian. Stress can also play a part, so check all the aquarium conditions.

KEEPING THE SUBSTRATE CLEAN

In addition to maintaining good water quality, it is also important to keep your substrate clean. There is some evidence that dirty gravel or gravel rich in decaying organic matter fosters the outbreak of bacterial infections. This particularly applies to diseases such as mouth rot or mouth fungus and the types of bacterial illness that can affect the mouths and barbels of catfish species.

◀ *When you see the first signs of infection, you may need to start treatment right away. Depending on the location and opening hours of your nearest aquatic shop, it may be a good idea to keep common medications in stock. Ensure you have basic antiparasite, antibacterial, and antifungal treatments readily available, as well as plenty of dechlorinator for emergency water changes.*

* *Carbon removes most medications from the water, so remove it from the filter while using a treatment in the tank. Afterward, replacing carbon will help to eliminate all traces of the medication from your setup.*

TANK CAPACITY

You need to know the capacity of your aquarium when using medications. Length (L) x Width (W) x Depth (D) in inches (cm) divided by 231 (1,000) will give you the volume in gallons (liters). Gravel and ornaments will displace water; reduce the volume by approximately 10 percent to allow for this.

▶ *Some medications can reduce oxygen levels in the water, and others can irritate the fish's gills. Some do both. For these reasons, it is important to ensure adequate aeration for the duration of a treatment. Add an extra power head or air pump to create surface movement.*

FISH PROFILES

Faced with the wide range of aquarium fish available at your local dealer, you may find it difficult to make a choice. On the following pages, you will find a selection of fish presented in categories to help you create suitable community aquariums (examples of which are featured on pages 82–95). The first group to be featured are so-called starter fish that are adaptable and hardy. These are the foundation for any mixed community aquarium. The next three sections look at peaceful small fish, medium-size fish, and large specimen fish. To house the larger fish, it is important to consider the size of the aquarium and its associated life-support systems.

Many fish naturally live in different zones within their habitats, and these are represented in the aquarium trade by those that live near the substrate, those that shoal in midwater, and those that spend most of their time at the water surface. Fish from these three zone categories are discussed next, followed by a look in turn at popular fish, active fish, and character fish. The last category includes those that are particularly striking or have a distinctive lifestyle. The selection of community fish closes with a look at algae eaters—always a useful function in any aquarium—and a brief look at the popular cichlids from the Rift Valley Lakes of East Africa.

All aquarium fish have both a common and a scientific name. Some fish may have several different common names but never more than one scientific name. When you buy fish for the first time, you will need to know the correct scientific name so you can choose the right fish. When you add fish to your aquarium, you should know the scientific names of the fish you already have so that you can check that any new ones are compatible with your existing stock.

▲ *Here a community of fish flourishes at all levels in a well-planted aquarium.*

Starter fish

A new aquarium takes time to establish, as bacteria colonize the filter to remove pollutants; water conditions, such as pH levels, stabilize; and both fish keeper and fish adjust to feeding regimes. Starter fish are naturally hardy, good-natured species that cope well with fluctuating conditions and are confident enough to settle into a tank with no other inhabitants. They live in a range of water conditions and do not require any special care. Once they are well established, the next group of fish can be introduced into a more balanced environment, gaining confidence from the presence of settled fish.

◀ *Keep the peaceful golden barb (Puntius semifasciolatus) in a group of five or six individuals. It is a lively, butter-colored species with varying amounts of black markings. Golden barbs will feel at home among dense vegetation.*

▲ *The Buenos Aires tetra (Puntius semifasciolatus) has a tendency to fin nip, but as long as you avoid keeping it with long-finned tankmates, it is ideal for a community aquarium. This hardy and adaptable species does not like water above 78.8°F (26°C) and makes a good tankmate for other temperate fish. Keep these peaceful, shoaling tetras in groups of four or more.*

OTHER STARTER FISH

Many barb, danio, and rainbow fish species are hardy and adaptable, including the platy, glowlight danio, zebra danio, rosy barb, and Lake Kutubu rainbow fish. Monitor water conditions carefully after introducing the first fish to your aquarium.

▶ *The White Cloud Mountain minnow* (Tanichthys albonubes) *is a peaceful, shoaling, and active fish that appreciates cooler water. It is best kept in groups of at least four, with other small tankmates.*

Female White Clouds are plumper and less brightly colored than males.

◀ *The extremely hardy and colorful paradise fish* (Macropodus opercularis) *is easy to maintain in a community tank with same-size and equally robust species. Since males are inclined to fight and even be aggressive toward the females, keep only one pair in any tank, and avoid mixing males together.*

STARTER FISH

▼ *The bloodfin tetra* (Aphyocharax anisitsi) *is a tough little fish that prefers to swim at the top of the aquarium, so provide some shelter with tall or floating plants. The bright red fins that give the fish its common name will show best once specimens are established and well settled.*

This young fish has yet to develop its full fin color.

Peaceful small fish

Although big tanks and big fish can be impressive, part of the enjoyment of fish keeping is observation, and smaller species can draw the eye just as much. Many small fish have intricate markings and shapes, and their characters make them perfectly suited for aquarium life. Smaller fish are also more peaceful than most, since their size reduces any effective form of aggression; even so, occasional squabbles may ensue.

* Most small fish are best kept in pairs or groups and need an aquarium with plenty of hiding spots and vegetation.

▲ *The mostly inoffensive and peaceful croaking gourami* (Trichopsis vittata) *is found in many color forms and in large numbers all over Southeast Asia. It is hardy and easy to keep and breed, and the fry are straightforward to rear. Males and females measure 2.5 in. (7 cm).*

TALKING FISH

The croaking gourami produces a clearly audible sound by rapidly fanning its pectoral fins, which causes the muscles to vibrate, while the labyrinth organ acts as a sound chamber. Keeping pairs or groups in the aquarium is fine; if more than one male is present, there are many more opportunities to hear the croaking sound made by both sexes.

▲ *The honey gourami* (Trichogaster chuna) *is an easy-to-keep and rewarding little gourami, ideal for the smaller community aquarium. At 1.5 in. (4 cm), males are slightly smaller and more colorful than females, especially at spawning time. The fish will spawn in the aquarium.*

◀ *Cherry barbs (Puntius titteya) do not naturally form shoals, so keep them as pairs in the aquarium. The color of the male in breeding condition inspires the fish's common name, but females are drabber. Both sexes measure 1 in. (5 cm).*

Few aquarium fish have a red color as intense as that of the male cherry barb.

▶ *The larger the shoal of checkered barbs (Puntius oligolepis), the more the males will show off their spawning colors to prospective partners. Although the fish are active and boisterous with their own kind, they are harmless to other tankmates.*

Five-banded barbs thrive in a group of five or six.

▼ *The very undemanding five-banded barb (Puntius pentazona) is ideal for the beginner. It grows to 2 in. (5 cm). Settled fish will sport reflective scales.*

PEACEFUL SMALL FISH

Peaceful small fish (continued)

Small fish need not always be kept in small tanks, but if they are, then you must exercise a little extra vigilance. Without a large volume of water to even out any changes, small tanks are more prone to fluctuations in water conditions. Regular water monitoring is essential, and maintenance, such as water changes, should be carried out on a little-and-often basis. Small fish tend to be opportunistic feeders, eating a wide range of food types in the wild. In the aquarium, provide a variety of small dried, frozen, or live foods.

◀ *Although other pencilfish require soft water, the golden pencilfish* (Nannostomus beckfordi) *will adapt to most conditions. Keep these relatively quiet and slow-moving fish in groups of six or more with similarly peaceful tankmates.*

* In a tank with densely planted areas and a dark substrate, the pencilfish's red body coloration will intensify. Established specimens look much more attractive than when you first acquire them.

Male red wagtail platy

▲ *The southern platy* (Xiphophorus maculatus) *is the perfect community fish, being peaceful, adaptable, and not a fussy eater. It has been hybridized with swordtails to produce the myriad color and fin forms seen in the trade.*

Female tuxedo platy

◀ *One of the smallest known fish, the dwarf, or pygmy, rasbora* (Boraras maculatus), *grows to a maximum size of just 1 in. (2.5 cm). With its small size and preference for slightly soft, acidic water, it is suited only to certain aquariums and communities.*

▶ *At just about 1 in. (2–3 cm) long, the pygmy corydoras* (Corydoras pygmaeus) *is ideally suited to a small aquarium. These peaceful corys are by nature shoaling fish, but they have a tendency to swim in groups in midwater, especially if there are other small fish to shoal with. They are best kept in ratios of two males to one female in a group of 12.*

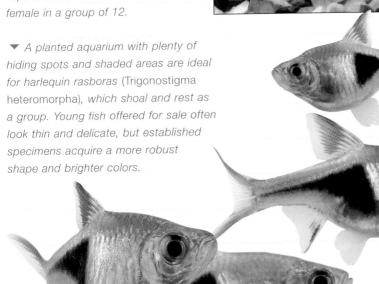

▼ *A planted aquarium with plenty of hiding spots and shaded areas are ideal for harlequin rasboras* (Trigonostigma heteromorpha), *which shoal and rest as a group. Young fish offered for sale often look thin and delicate, but established specimens acquire a more robust shape and brighter colors.*

Distinctive markings allow this fish to stand out, despite its small size.

PEACEFUL SMALL FISH

MEDIUM-SIZE FISH

Medium-size fish

A range of different-size fish will create a lively, mixed display, and a few medium-size species can be used as specimen fish in a community of smaller species. Alternatively, these fish are large enough to be seen from a distance, and when several are kept together, the aquarium becomes a more active feature viewed from any part of a room. The gouramis and cichlids featured here can be slow-moving and graceful as well as territorial fish with aggressive tendencies. To create a peaceful community of fish such as these, it is important to keep them in the right numbers.

◀ *The ghostly moonlight gourami* (Trichogaster microlepis) *can become the target of fin-nipping fish, so keep it with peaceful species. Provide this timid fish with the cover offered by dense planting. It grows up to 6 in. (15 cm). Moonlights stand out because of their plain color.*

SPAWNING BEHAVIOR

Most gouramis build floating 'nests' of bubbles between plants at the surface, where eggs are deposited after spawning. The bubblenests may include bits of plant material, so plenty of vegetation in the aquarium will encourage spawning.

▼ *The flowing fins and shimmering colors of the male pearl gourami* (Trichogaster leeri) *will enhance virtually any community tank. Both sexes grow to 4.75 in. (12 cm). Keep the fish in pairs or trios (one male to two females); they will spawn in the aquarium.*

Pearl gouramis can be quite long lived in the aquarium, surviving for up to eight years.

◀ *The extremely hardy and robust three spot, or opaline, gourami (Trichogaster trichopterus) adapts to almost any water conditions and has become one of the most common gouramis for the community tank. Keep one pair or one trio (one male to two females). This species can be a little spiteful toward other fish and aggressive during spawning.*

Female

Male

▲ *Although many cichlids can be aggressive, the rainbow cichlid (Herotilapia multispinosa) is relatively mild-mannered and will do well in a community of larger fish. These fish like to hang around the lower regions and will appreciate caves made from rocks or wood.*

◀ *The angel (Pterophyllum scalare) is so unusual in shape that most people do not realize it is a cichlid at all. It is available in numerous man-made forms, varying in both color and finnage. Even when breeding, it is a very peaceful species. Males and females can grow to about 5 in. (13 cm) long and rather more deep but are usually smaller. They are natural shoalers, so keep them in a group in the aquarium.*

MEDIUM-SIZE FISH

MEDIUM-SIZE FISH

Medium-size fish (continued)

Mollies, swordtails, and rainbow fish are more colorful and active than gouramis and cichlids and ideal for a display with plenty of movement. All the fish featured here are surface feeders that thrive on floating foods such as flake but develop the best colors if fed a varied diet containing some live or frozen supplements. Gouramis, angelfish and cichlids are naturally soft-water fish, whereas mollies, swordtails, and rainbow fish come from harder water. Most species for sale are tank-bred and do well in medium to hard water.

◀ A distinctive stripe marks this medium-size cichlid, which is found in the same natural habitats as angelfish and discus. Although peaceful, the festive cichlid (Mesonauta festivus) does have minor territorial tendencies, so allow at least 24 in. (60 cm) of tank length for one pair.

▶ Good filtration and high-quality water are very important to keep the striking sailfin molly (Poecilia velifera) in good condition. Wild fish have been hybridized with Poecilia latipinna and other mollies to produce many color varieties.

Green sailfin molly

Orange sailfin molly

▶ This silver lyretail may have been crossed with other molly species.

The pineapple sword's markings are closest to the wild form.

◀ Cultivated swordtails (Xiphophorus helleri) *are very hardy fish. A spacious community aquarium containing other robust species will suit swordtails, which are boisterous and active. They behave well, as long as they are not allowed to dominate. Females measure 4.75 in. (12 cm), males 3 in. (8 cm) (excluding the sword).*

The huge variety of color types will brighten any tank.

These fish are males; females do not have the distinctive sword-shaped tail fin.

▶ Boeseman's rainbow fish (Melanotaenia boesemani) *is a popular and beautiful species, but males do not attain their full colors until they are about 12 months old. Keep this very active shoaling fish in a tank with gentle water movement, and provide a well-fitting cover, as it is a good jumper.*

◀ Lake Kutubu rainbow fish (Melano-taenia lacustris), *also known as the blue rainbow fish, will show their colors while still relatively young. If you observe patiently, you can see that the head area of many rainbow fish changes color within seconds when they become excitable, which is known as flashing.*

Large specimen fish

Large fish need large tanks, and most of these species will need an aquarium measuring at least 60 in. (150 cm)—more if it is to house several fish. Think carefully before taking on such a large display. However, if you have the room, the fish make excellent show specimens and will become quite tame with their owners. One problem with big fish is that they can be a little boisterous and will probably destroy plants, so limit the decor to large objects that are not easily moved or liable to break the glass if knocked.

◀ *Being shoaling fish, silver sharks* (Balantiocheilus melanopterus) *should be kept in threes or more. Males and females grow to 12 in. (30 cm), and such a group would need a sizable tank measuring 60 in. (150 cm). Apart from this, the fish are easy to care for, are active and peaceful, can be kept with smaller fish, and are good community tankmates for other active, robust fish.*

* Tinfoil barbs are avid plant eaters and are usually kept in very large, relatively bare display tanks with other peaceful community fish that outgrow normal community aquariums.

The tinfoil barb gets its common name from the highly reflective silver scales that glisten under bright light.

▶ *The tinfoil barb* (Barbonymus schwanenfeldii) *is a peaceful, active shoaler (keep at least two together) but is not to be trusted with fish smaller than 2 in. (5 cm), which it will regard as live food. Do not be fooled by the cute juveniles offered for sale; the deep-bodied tinfoil barb will grow to an impressive 12 in. (30 cm) and needs a correspondingly deep tank if it is to thrive.*

▼ *The beautifully patterned tiger shovelnose catfish (Merodontotus tigrinus) grows to 20 in. (50 cm) and needs a large aquarium equipped with a powerful filter system that can create the highly oxygenated, fast-moving water it enjoys in the wild. This very expensive fish is a predator that should be kept only with other large species.*

The shovelnose is an active fish and easily spooked — a large tank is essential to prevent the fish from crashing into the glass and damaging its sensitive nose.

◀ *The common plec (Hypostomus sp.) is a hardy fish and a great algae eater, but it can be destructive and messy and will damage plants. Despite its potential size of up to 18 in. (45 cm), it will live happily with fish of any size.*

▼ *The banded leporinus (Leporinus fasciatus) makes an active and interesting addition to a community aquarium with sizable and robust but peaceful tankmates. Males and females grow to 12 in. (30 cm) and appreciate a tank furnished with large pieces of bogwood and a sandy substrate. Provide good filtration and areas of strong flow.*

* This strikingly patterned fish belongs to the headstander group, although it only occasionally displays the distinctive head-down resting position.

Contrasting markings and a distinctive torpedo shape make this fish stand out.

Large specimen fish (continued)

Large fish produce considerable quantities of waste, which can cloud the water and cause conditions to deteriorate if the correct filtration is not installed. Large external filters are essential, housing mechanical media such as sponges to trap and remove debris. Regular large water changes, carried out in conjunction with gravel cleaning, may be required to keep nitrate levels low, so it will help to have a storage area where water can be prepared for use in the aquarium.

▶ *The round body of the silver dollar (Metynnis argenteus) gives it a strong presence in the aquarium, where a group will make excellent tankmates for other large peaceful fish and even some larger cichlids. Silver dollars are exclusively vegetarian, so feed them with pellet food, herbivorous flake, algae wafers, lettuce, cucumber, and plant matter.*

When in spawning condition, the fins will become brighter and markings may appear on the body.

◀ *This is a juvenile uaru (Uaru amphiacanthoides). Uarus have endearing character and are easy to keep in groups. A shoal will relish the addition of plants or lettuce leaves, which they will quickly devour.*

▶ *The oscar (Astronotus ocellatus) is arguably the best known and most popular large cichlid and soon learns to recognize its owner. It grows to 10–16 in. (25–40 cm) and can be kept in a single-species tank or with a large armored catfish (plec) as a scavenger. Use large, securely placed decor and heater guards, and glue smaller decorations in place so the fish cannot move or damage them.*

◀ *The adult severum (Heros severus) is a graceful presence in larger tanks and will become quite confident, although young juveniles may be timid and nervous when first introduced to a new environment. A gold variety is popular, but adults of the green or wild variety sport more interesting markings.*

▶ *Growing to an impressive 16 in. (40 cm), the long-nose distichodus (Distichodus lusosso) requires a large aquarium. In the wild, it grazes on algae growing on rocks, and a brightly lit aquarium will encourage a supply of this vegetarian food.*

▶ *D. sexfasciatus is very similar but can be aggressive, and its color will fade with age. The two can be distinguished by the shape of the nose.*

Substrate dwellers

Substrate dwellers play an important part in the aquarium. As well as occupying the lower region of the display, they help keep it clean, as their scavenging removes waste food particles, and their turning over gravel prevents the algae from establishing. Avoid using sharp gravel, which can damage sensitive mouthparts, and feed substrate dwellers on a range of sinking foods, as they will not survive on leftovers. Providing a few cavelike hiding places and some vegetation will help them feel at home.

◀ *The Asian striped catfish* (Mystus vittatus) *is a shoaling species, and a group of seven or eight specimens in a large planted aquarium is an impressive sight.*

The Asian striped catfish has four distinctive, thick, dark candy stripes running the full length of the body, giving it a very sleek appearance.

NAKED CATFISH

Mystus vittatus is a naked catfish meaning there are no scales or scutes to protect the body. The skin is quite tough but is easily scratched or damaged by sharp objects. Always use tank decorations and furnishings with smooth edges.

Corydoras adolfoi is just one of the many cory species, each with its own intricate markings.

Corydoras sterbai has orange pectoral fins — a good indicator that it can release toxins when stressed.

▶ Corydoras *catfish are small, peaceful, hardy, and full of character. Keep at least three or four of any single species.*

▶ The beautiful emerald catfish (Brochis splendens) spends most of its time with its nose buried in the sandy substrate searching for food. Keep the fish in a group of six. Juveniles display a greatly exaggerated dorsal fin and are often imported as sailfin corys.

▼ The dwarf chain loach (Botia sidthimunki) is adaptable and active during the day, scavenging the aquarium substrate for food items. These very sociable fish are best kept in groups of three or more. Provide a few hiding spots and a varied diet, including sinking pellets, wafers, and live or frozen foods.

The black markings along the length of this fish give it its common name.

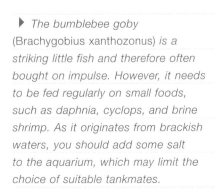

▶ The bumblebee goby (Brachygobius xanthozonus) is a striking little fish and therefore often bought on impulse. However, it needs to be fed regularly on small foods, such as daphnia, cyclops, and brine shrimp. As it originates from brackish waters, you should add some salt to the aquarium, which may limit the choice of suitable tankmates.

Shoaling midwater fish

Fish have good reasons to stick together in the wild; in most cases, it is a good strategy to follow others in order to find food quickly and escape dangers such as predators more rapidly. In the aquarium, a shoal normally consists of about six fish, although if there is room, greater numbers will make a more effective display. Small shoaling fish will display confidence and their best colors only if they are aware of the aquarium's safe areas, so provide some areas of dense vegetation, decor, or hiding spots.

* *Other species use shoaling fish as a sign that it is safe for them to swim out into the open. Notice heightened activity, which may indicate feeding times.*

▼ *In the right water conditions (soft and slightly acidic), the rummy-nose tetra (Hemigrammus bleheri) sports a striking red coloration around the head and distinctive tail fin stripes. Keep these peaceful fish in groups of five or more. Although they appreciate hiding places among the plants, they will spend time in the open.*

▶ *The silver tip tetra (Hasemania nana) is an excellent community fish, especially for new aquariums. It is hardy and adaptable, and because it is a confident open-water swimmer, it will encourage more delicate, timid fish to venture out as well.*

▶ *Keep the threadfin rainbow fish* (Iriatherina werneri) *in groups of five or more. At 2 in. (5 cm), the males are larger and more colorful than females and have long threadlike extensions on the dorsal and anal fins, which they use to display to each other. These attractive fish are well suited to the smaller aquarium.*

◀ *The bold-looking red-eye tetra* (Moenkhausia sanctaefilomenae) *also has a distinctive black band across the tail and dark-edged scales that give it an almost armor-plated appearance. It swims toward the surface, as well as in midwater, and enjoys the cover of a well-planted aquarium. Keep in a shoal of five to six fish.*

▶ *A relatively new addition to the aquarium hobby, the glowlight danio* (Danio choprai), *looks set to become a popular fish. It is an active surface-shoaling species, with orange and red markings that are bright and distinctive, especially for a fish that grows to only about 1.5 in. (3.5 cm) long.*

SURFACE DWELLERS

Surface dwellers

In nature, the water surface is a good place to find food. This is where bugs and insects fall into the water and where fruits and seeds drop from overhanging vegetation. Most surface dwellers are accustomed to shallow, vegetated areas, such as stream banks or the shallow edges of larger rivers, so they may become unsettled if kept in aquariums without any hiding areas at the surface. Floating plants, tall plants, and tall pieces of bogwood all make good hiding areas. Floating food is essential for surface dwellers, as only a few will swim down to feed. Even though they live at the surface, they are often slow to feed, so make sure they get sufficient food by spreading out the feeding area or distracting other fish with sinking foods.

▲ The common hatchetfish (Gasteropelecus sternicla) *is often confused with the silver hatchetfish, which has a deeper throat. Common hatchetfish are robust and if given a few suitable hiding spots at the surface, will become confident and well-mannered fish.*

GOOD JUMPERS

The odd shape of the hatchetfish is due to an enlarged muscle that allows it to jump above the water surface and travel several yards (meters) to avoid danger. Because of this well-developed escape response, these fish remain constantly at the surface, and a good lid is essential to prevent them jumping from the tank.

▶ *The black-winged hatchetfish* (Carnegiella marthae) *is quiet and peaceful and does not bother other fish, making it an ideal addition to a community aquarium. Keep this shoaling fish in a group of at least three individuals.*

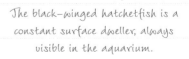

The black-winged hatchetfish is a constant surface dweller, always visible in the aquarium.

◀ *In a community of similar-size fish, the halfbeak (Dermogenys pusilla) will prove a peaceful addition. Provide a diet of mosquito larvae, fruit flies, and other live foods. It will take flake and frozen foods, but not from the bottom of the tank.*

▼ *The sparkling panchax (Aplocheilus lineatus) is a very easy-to-keep, top-swimming fish with a large wide mouth that appears to be permanently smiling! It lives happily in the upper part of the aquarium, providing color and movement among the floating plants.*

▲ *A number of surface-swimming killifish, including A. lineatus, have developed a shiny scale on the top of the head. Flies and insects tempted by the shiny scale quickly become a ready meal.*

The butterfly fish lives up to its common name in appearance.

◀ *With its straight back, upturned mouth, and superb camouflage, the butterfly fish (Pantodon buchholzi) has all the qualities needed to be an efficient predator of small, surface-swimming fish. Keep a group of three to six in a heavily planted aquarium with similar-size, bottom- to middle-dwelling species.*

POPULAR FISH

Popular fish

There are many highly popular aquarium fish in the hobby. They are available in any store throughout the year, and their bright colors draw the newcomer's eye. Nevertheless, these fish are not always ideal for new fish keepers, and many suffer from problems associated with intensive captive breeding or line breeding to produce new color types. It is easy to buy such fish on impulse, but do your research first. Even the universally known guppy has its problems when included in a community aquarium.

▶ *The dwarf gourami (Colisa lalia) is one of the most popular and attractive aquarium fish. Several color forms are available, enhancing the reds and blues in the natural coloration of wild-caught fish.*

The red dwarf variant is quite unlike the wild striped species.

Male cobalt blue dwarf gourami

Female cobalt blue dwarf gourami

▶ *Once established in a mature aquarium with good water conditions, the neon tetra (Paracheirodon innesi) proves hardy and robust. For the best visual effect, keep a large group together. Avoid tankmates large enough to eat these small tetras, and keep them with other peaceful fish.*

Under good lighting, the neons' scales will appear reflective.

* *Most specimens of neon tetra are mass bred and now show signs of weakness associated with extensive breeding. Check for good color and body shape when buying these fish.*

◄ *The cardinal tetra (Paracheirodon axelrodi) can be distinguished from the neon tetra by the red and blue bars that extend along the whole body in the cardinal. In recent years, cardinals have become a more popular alternative to the neon, and good specimens can be hardier than some weak stocks of neons.*

* Cardinal tetras look best when kept in large groups of 10–20 or more, space permitting.

▶ *The delightful ram, or butterfly dwarf cichlid, (Microgeophagus ramirezi) is a peaceful fish, even when breeding. It requires very soft, slightly acid water for long-term survival and breeding. Home-bred stock is more expensive but well worth the extra outlay.*

Male

Female

◄ *The popularity of the krib (Pelvicachromis pulcher) is not hard to explain; it is a small, colorful, fairly peaceful cichlid that is easy to keep, sex, and breed. Brood care is excellent and continues for many months.*

POPULAR FISH

POPULAR FISH

Popular fish (continued)

Most popular fish are tank-bred and acclimated to a retailer's local water conditions, so will not require any special treatment. While most of these fish prefer to be in groups, some, such as the red-tailed black shark, are loners. Never keep two of them together, as this will result in constant fights for territory. Most popular fish are relatively peaceful, but do not take this for granted. Livebearers, such as the guppy and molly, should be kept in a ratio of two females to every male, to dampen the effect of constant male attention, while cichlids such as the kribensis and ram are best in pairs.

POSSIBLE PROBLEMS

Although guppies are easy to keep and breed in a well-maintained aquarium, most specimens for sale are heavily bred, leading to a low disease tolerance. Their long fins also make a good target for fin-nipping fish, and this limits the choice of fish that you can add to

▶ *The guppy (Poecilia reticulata) is a lively, colorful, and peaceful community fish. The mottled markings give the variety shown here the name of leopard, or mosaic, guppy.*

Female

Male

◀ *The black molly (Poecilia sphenops) makes a lively addition to the middle and upper water levels of a roomy community display. Its placid nature means it will coexist with all other peaceful species. Provide a well-planted tank and medium hard water, with a pH of 7 to 7.4.*

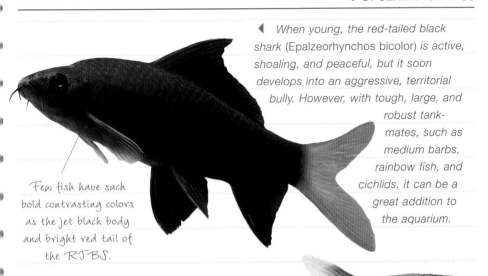

◀ *When young, the red-tailed black shark (Epalzeorhynchos bicolor) is active, shoaling, and peaceful, but it soon develops into an aggressive, territorial bully. However, with tough, large, and robust tank-mates, such as medium barbs, rainbow fish, and cichlids, it can be a great addition to the aquarium.*

Few fish have such bold contrasting colors as the jet black body and bright red tail of the RTBS.

▶ *Being hardy, peaceful, and small, the glowlight tetra (Hemigrammus erythrozonus) meets all the criteria for a small community fish. Keep these attractive fish in groups of at least five. Regular feeds will keep them in top condition, and darker decor will bring out their bright colors.*

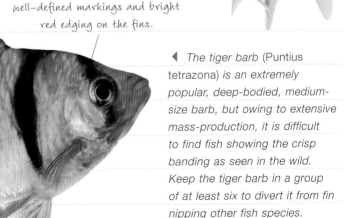

Established tiger barbs will show well-defined markings and bright red edging on the fins.

◀ *The tiger barb (Puntius tetrazona) is an extremely popular, deep-bodied, medium-size barb, but owing to extensive mass-production, it is difficult to find fish showing the crisp banding as seen in the wild. Keep the tiger barb in a group of at least six to divert it from fin nipping other fish species.*

ACTIVE FISH

Active fish

Whereas slow-moving, peaceful species can be relaxing, a lively dynamic aquarium stocked with active species can create a more stimulating display. Active fish are almost all shoaling fish, continually chasing each other, searching for food, and appearing to play throughout the aquarium. They often recognize the fish keeper and will excitedly come to the front of the aquarium if they think it might be feeding time. Not all fish enjoy such a boisterous environment, so active species are best kept with fish of a similar nature.

◀ *The striking coloration of Denison's barb (Puntius denisonii) stands out in the aquarium. Although it can be expensive and needs a roomy tank, it is an excellent, active aquarium fish.*

▶ *The undemanding rosy barb* (Puntius conchonius) *is a long-lived, very hardy species, with normal and long-finned forms. The fish show their best colors over a dark substrate. Keep at least two, but ideally a small shoal, in a planted tank.*

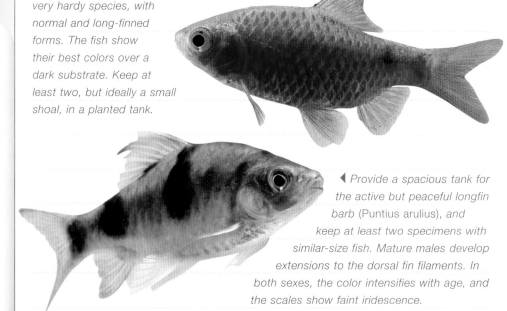

◀ *Provide a spacious tank for the active but peaceful longfin barb* (Puntius arulius), *and keep at least two specimens with similar-size fish. Mature males develop extensions to the dorsal fin filaments. In both sexes, the color intensifies with age, and the scales show faint iridescence.*

▶ *The Congo tetra (Phenacogrammus interruptus) is an excellent shoaling fish for larger tanks and communities of medium-size fish. The fish like to swim in the open in the middle to upper areas of the tank. Keep a group of at least five, and avoid aggressive tankmates.*

The iridescent blues and yellows show up best in established specimens.

Male Congo tetras have long ragged fins that flow in the water.

Gold giant danio

The streamlined, torpedo body is a good indicator that this is a fast-moving fish.

Giant danio

▲ *As its common name suggests, the giant danio (Danio aequipinnatus) is one of the largest danios commonly available, growing up to 5 in. (12 cm). These hardy and adaptable fish make good tankmates for a lively aquarium of similar-size fish. Because of its constant movement, avoid delicate tankmates.*

* When buying giant danios, check that the mouth shape is intact, as young fish can be easily spooked and often knock themselves on the glass, damaging the mouth.

ACTIVE FISH

ACTIVE FISH

Active fish (continued)

Many active fish are naturally hardy, originating as they do from fast-flowing waters and streams where water conditions may change with the seasons or throughout the day. They are quite adaptable to differing ranges of pH and hardness but also require good filtration, oxygenation, and ideally, areas of water movement. Since active fish are messy feeders, add scavenging fish to the aquarium to clean up the leftovers. Most loaches are ideal for this purpose, since they are also naturally active fish.

◀ *Although not overly colorful, the distinctive tail markings of the scissortail rasbora (Rasbora trilineata) add movement and interest to a community aquarium of similar-size tankmates. Keep the fish in groups of four or more, and provide plenty of swimming space, along with hiding places and vegetation around the edges.*

▶ *The zebra danio (Danio rerio) is often recommended as a first fish due to its hardy, peaceful, and confident nature. A group of at least four will add a great deal of movement to the aquarium and liven up any display.*

This is the normal form of zebra danio — long-finned and albino varieties are also common.

◀ *Some people believe that the leopard danio is a separate species (Danio frankei), while others think it is a color morph of the zebra danio. Both are ideal for a small community aquarium.*

ACTIVE FISH

◀ *Its active and playful nature makes the zebra loach (Botia striata) an interesting addition to the community aquarium. Keep this peaceful and very sociable fish in groups of at least three. Because of its constant scavenging activity, a sandy or smooth substrate is essential; otherwise, it will damage its sensitive barbels.*

▲ *To appreciate the striking pictus catfish (Pimelodus pictus) at its active best, provide plenty of swimming space so that it can move around freely. In addition to its silver body, black spots, and elegant lines, the fish has very long barbels that it uses constantly to feel its way around.*

* *Although active fish need plenty of open swimming spaces, they also like to be stimulated by their environment, so include areas of robust vegetation and decor around the back and sides of the aquarium.*

◀ *The dwarf rainbow fish (Melanotaenia praecox) is a peaceful, active shoaling fish, ideal for the smaller community aquarium. Keep at least one pair together, but a group of five would make a good show of color. Males have red fins and a blue sheen to the body, and females are silver with yellow-orange fins.*

CHARACTER FISH

Character fish

New fish keepers are often surprised by the diversity of character and behavior seen in aquarium fish. A character fish often becomes its owner's favorite and the one that most visitors notice. Such fish may be exceptionally lively, be inquisitive, or have unusual physical characteristics. The unusual swimming habits of the upside-down catfish and spotted headstander, excellent navigation of the blind cave tetra, and stunning color and finnage of the Siamese fighting fish are all characteristics that make fish keeping such an interesting pursuit.

▶ *With its wonderful colors and flowing fins, the popular Siamese fighting fish* (Betta splendens) *makes an interesting addition to a community aquarium with small, peaceful tankmates that will not nip at the male's trailing fins.*

ONE MALE PER TANK

Male Siamese fighting fish *(Betta splendens)* are generally fairly docile unless they come across another male, in which they case they will actively fight. Although you should never keep more than one male in a community, it is safe to house a pair or one male to several females to suit the size of the tank.

* Like all anabantoids, the Siamese fighting fish has an auxiliary breathing organ (the labyrinth organ) that enables it to breathe atmospheric air at the water surface.

▶ *Given its very poor eyesight, the port hoplo catfish* (Megalechis thoracata) *depends on its sensitive barbels to explore its surroundings, which it does continually, sometimes to the annoyance of other fish. It is this activity that makes the fish so interesting to observe in the aquarium.*

* Many *Synodontis* species are referred to as upside-down catfish, but this one is considered to be the original and is even recorded in ancient Egyptian wall carvings.

◀ *In the wild, the inverted swimming habit of the upside-down catfish (Synodontis nigriventris) enables it to feed on mosquito larvae that gather at the water surface or under overhanging leaves and submerged vegetation. In the aquarium, it will accept tablet, flake, and frozen foods, as well as bloodworms, daphnia, and mosquito larvae.*

▶ *Despite having no vision, the blind cave tetra (Astyanax mexicanus) uses highly developed senses, also present in other characins, to locate food and navigate. In its natural cave habitat, the fish does not need to see, but interestingly the fry have fully functional eyes, which become covered as the fish mature.*

Working eyes covered by skin.

◀ *The spotted headstander (Chilodus punctatus) lives up to its common name by resting in a head down position. Keep these peaceful and somewhat timid fish in small groups with other peaceful species, and provide some vegetable matter in their diet.*

CHARACTER FISH

Character fish (continued)

Unusual fish appear in nature when specific environments drive their evolution, which means they often have specific requirements in the aquarium. For this reason you should always think carefully and do your research before buying a character fish. Discus, for example, require specific water conditions and high-quality source water; clown and kuhli loaches need a soft, sandy substrate; and glass catfish require flowing water. For any aquarium, there is a character fish that will fit in well with the other inhabitants, providing it is chosen with its needs in mind.

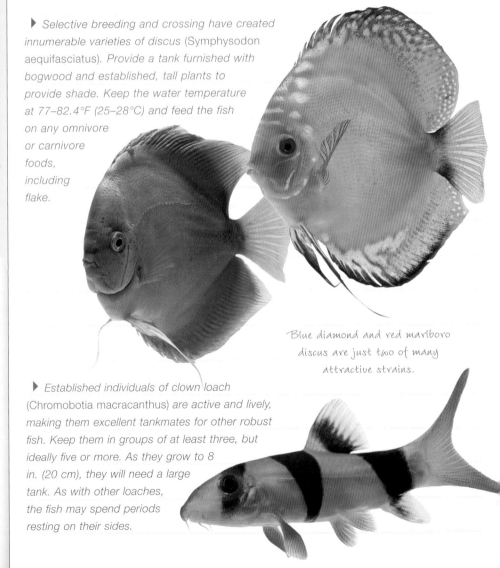

▶ *Selective breeding and crossing have created innumerable varieties of discus* (Symphysodon aequifasciatus). *Provide a tank furnished with bogwood and established, tall plants to provide shade. Keep the water temperature at 77–82.4°F (25–28°C) and feed the fish on any omnivore or carnivore foods, including flake.*

Blue diamond and red marlboro discus are just two of many attractive strains.

▶ *Established individuals of clown loach* (Chromobotia macracanthus) *are active and lively, making them excellent tankmates for other robust fish. Keep them in groups of at least three, but ideally five or more. As they grow to 8 in. (20 cm), they will need a large tank. As with other loaches, the fish may spend periods resting on their sides.*

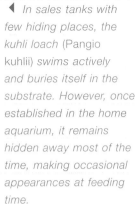

◀ *In sales tanks with few hiding places, the kuhli loach (Pangio kuhlii) swims actively and buries itself in the substrate. However, once established in the home aquarium, it remains hidden away most of the time, making occasional appearances at feeding time.*

Provide this burrowing fish with soft or rounded substrates that will not damage its barbels.

◀ *One of nature's little wonders is the archerfish (Toxotes jaculatrix), which gets its common name from its ability to accurately shoot insects off overhanging branches by firing jets of water from its mouth. In the aquarium, these fish can grow up to 10 in. (25 cm), so they will need a large tank. They prefer brackish water.*

▶ *A see-through body is not to everyone's taste, but the glass catfish (Kryptopterus bicirrhis) is a unique species to observe. Keep these timid fish in groups, and provide a varied diet of flake and live or frozen foods.*

ALGAE EATERS

Algae eaters

Fish that remove algae from the aquarium are obviously very useful and are often acquired simply for this trait, without a thought for their specific needs or their contribution to a community as interesting species in their own right. Many a fish keeper has experienced the problems associated with the de facto algae eater, the common plec, which soon grows too large for most aquariums and becomes a destructive pest. The algae eaters featured here will all do their job but are also worthwhile and manageable species.

* Mature males have longer, branched, soft bristles down the center and around the sides of the head. Females are said to choose to mate with the male with the best set of bristles.

▲ As well as browsing on the aquarium glass, the bristlenose catfish (Ancistrus *sp.*) grazes on soft bogwood.

The mouth is designed for both suction and rasping power, enabling it to graze algae while sticking to objects in fast-flowing water.

◀ At 4 in. (10 cm), the clown plec (Peckoltia vittata) is the ideal suckermouth catfish for all but the smallest displays. It browses on any algae growing on plant leaves and decor and also accepts tablet, wafer, and fresh green foods. Provide some hiding places in the aquarium.

◀ *Perched on even the smallest plant leaves or up against the glass, Otocinclus species grazes the entire aquarium of any algae (other than blue-green and brush). Given their constant browsing behavior, it is important to provide algae tablets and wafers when natural levels become low.*

Otocinclus catfish keep algae under control at all levels in the tank.

▼ *The sticklike body shape and coloration of the twig catfish (Farlowella acus) protect it from predation in the wild. Its movement is restricted by armor-plated scales along the body, and it never swims far. Feed these algae eaters on tablets and wafers, away from areas where other fish are feeding on flake food.*

▼ *For planted aquariums, there is nothing better than the algae shrimp (Caridina japonica) for removing algae. A group of shrimps will remove algae from the smallest of places without causing any damage to delicate plants. They will even remove hair, brush, and blue-green algae, which most algae-eating fish leave behind.*

ALGAE EATERS

Algae eaters (continued)

Many algae-eating fish require slightly soft water to thrive, so choose carefully if your aquarium has hard water. However, they are more demanding of the type of decor in the aquarium than of water conditions. Bogwood is an essential addition for many algae eaters. Some do not like bright light, so bogwood provides ideal hiding spots for them. But just as important, grazing on bogwood aids the natural digestive system of some algae eaters. Plants are also welcome; smaller algae eaters will not damage leaves during grazing, and the larger specimens can be kept with more robust plants.

◀ *Although young algae loaches (Gyrinocheilus aymonieri) are reasonably well behaved, mature specimens will chase and bully weaker fish. Despite this, they are a good addition to communities of larger, robust fish, including larger cichlids and barbs. Keep only one per tank, since they will fight with each other.*

POTENTIAL CONFUSION

There are several species that look similar to the Siamese flying fox, including the common flying fox, but these are neither as peaceful nor as good at eating algae. The Siamese flying fox can be identified by its stockier body, better-defined scales, clear fins, and the single black line that extends into the tail fin.

* Closely related fish, including sharks, algae loaches, and flying foxes, often squabble, but keeping five or more individuals normally keeps situations harmless.

▶ *The Siamese flying fox (Crossocheilus siamensis) is an excellent algae eater, even tackling the fibrous hair and brush algae that most other algae eaters leave behind. Having an active nature, it is a good tankmate for other sizable, robust fish in a community tank.*

◀ *Although it is a good algae eater, the ruby shark (Epalzeorhynchos frenatum) may damage some delicate foliage. Provide a varied diet that includes sinking pellets, algae wafers, and live and frozen foods. The ruby shark is a good alternative to the red-tailed black shark in a community aquarium.*

▶ *There are over 40 species of bulldog catfish (Chaetostoma sp.), and they are not easy to tell apart. Most will grow to 4–6 in. (10–15 cm) and prefer an aquarium with good filtration and water movement. Bulldog catfish enjoy grazing algae from smooth rocks and appreciate a few hiding places in caves of rocks or wood.*

◀ *The hillstream loach (Beaufortia leveretti) is a very interesting little algae eater, perfectly designed for sticking to objects in fast-flowing water. To keep these fish correctly, the aquarium must have plenty of water flow, so it is a good idea to install an additional pump. Provide a diet of algae wafers and small frozen or live foods.*

ALGAE EATERS

MALAWI CICHLIDS

Malawi cichlids

The cichlids of Lake Malawi include some of the most beautiful fish in the hobby, with bright yellow and electric blue being the most dominant colors. The cichlids can be roughly divided into two groups: open-water species and the rock-dwelling mbuna. The fish in this group are the ones most often seen in aquariums. Mbuna are naturally aggressive and territorial and will not mix with other types of aquarium fish, with the exception of a few hardy catfish species.

▶ *The common name of the Malawi blue dolphin cichlid* (Cyrtocara moorii) *relates to the dolphinlike head profile. It is a bottom dweller that does well in a Malawi community with other sand dwellers or open-water species, but not with rock-dwelling Malawi mbuna, which are far more aggressive. Keep no more than one male but as many females as desired.*

◀ *Trewavas's cichlid* (Labeotropheus trewavasae) *is one of the mbuna, the local name for the colorful rock dwellers of Lake Malawi. Keep it in a mbuna-only community aquarium, with no more than one male specimen and one or several females. It is relatively peaceful for an mbuna, and males rarely harass females.*

▶ *The melanochromis mbuna are regarded as the most aggressive Malawi cichlids, so keep only one in a Malawi community and do not introduce it until the aquarium is already well stocked. In large aquariums, over 59 in. (150 cm), it is possible to keep a male along with a couple of females, but in smaller tanks the male, or even a dominant female, may kill the weaker female.*

▶ *For a large tank with an area of open water, the venustus (Nimbochromis venustus) makes a stunning specimen fish, but it will grow up to 10 in. (25 cm). It is a natural predator, so avoid mixing it with smaller fish. Keep one male per tank. Several females can cohabit.*

The male venustus will develop an intense metallic blue face and bright yellow markings on the head.

* Malawi cichlids of the same groups will interbreed easily, and most specimens seen for sale may not be true species.

▲ *The zebra cichlid (Metriaclima zebra) will feel at home among vast amounts of rockwork that provide numerous caves. Keep it in an mbuna-only community aquarium, and provide an omnivore diet with plenty of vegetable matter and minimal amounts of dried food, which can lead to the fatal Malawi bloat.*

THE AQUARIUM

To re-create the natural conditions of Lake Malawi, the aquarium should have a dense rocky appearance and the water should be hard and alkaline. To keep aggression to a minimum, it is common practice to maintain a high stocking level to prevent the fish from establishing territories. This in turn requires strong filtration and regular water changes to cope with the high production of waste.

TANGANYIKAN CICHLIDS

Tanganyikan cichlids

The cichlids of Lake Tanganyika are more peaceful than those of Lake Malawi, but they can be equally territorial when breeding. For this reason you should avoid mixing them with peaceful species by keeping them in a Tanganyikan community. In contrast to the Malawi cichlids, which feed mainly on herbivorous material, Tanganyikan cichlids require a little more meat in their diet and appreciate regular supplements of frozen foods. As with Malawi cichlids, these fish prefer slightly hard, alkaline water.

◀ *Compressiceps (Altolamprologus compressiceps) is a very attractive, small, rock-dwelling cichlid with several geographical color variants. It has a tendency toward nervousness and stringent requirements with regard to water chemistry and quality. Feed this piscivore at dawn and dusk on a diet that includes raw fish as well as shrimp, prawn, earthworms, and carnivore pellets.*

* Tanganyikan cichlids have diverse spawning methods and are usually excellent parents, making them an interesting group of species for aquarium breeding.

▶ *The popular frontosa (Cyphotilapia frontosa) grows to a large size—males up to 8 in. (21 cm), females up to 6.75 in. (17 cm)—and will eat tankmates. It does best in groups or with other large, relatively peaceful Tanganyikan or Malawi cichlids.*

Julies are found in various parts of Lake Tanganyika and vary in appearance. This is the Kelimi form.

◀ *All the Julies—*Julido-chromis transcriptus—*are popular with aquarists because of their attractive appearance and interesting behavior. They are able to swim backward or on their sides/upside-down with their bellies toward the nearest rock. This small species is one of the easiest to keep and breed.*

▶ *The fairy cichlid* (Neolamprologus brichardi) *is elegant, readily available, and easy to keep. House a pair or, if the aquarium is large enough, a small group. If the fish breed, do not remove the young until they measure about 1 in. (2.5 cm), as they help guard the next broods. Adults may stop spawning if deprived of their families.*

◀ *The male and female lemon cichlid* (Neolamprologus leleupi) *are equally striking. They spawn in caves, with both parents showing brood care. Do not keep more than a single pair in tanks less than 59 in. (150 cm) long.*

COMMUNITY AQUARIUMS

This part of the book showcases a number of community aquarium mixes that you might like to try. It is important to appreciate the distinction between community fish and communities of fish. Although there are some fish that will happily live together in a mixed community aquarium, there are many others that can form the basis of communities defined by the lifestyle or environmental needs of the fish they support.

Each community mix is based around a tank of a certain size. The ingredients are arranged around a graphic of the tank and include a panel listing the fish suitable for the aquarium and the numbers of each species this size of tank will support once the system is stable. Arrows extending from the pictures of the fish indicate the approximate level that the fish occupies in the tank. Information on suitable plants and decor is also provided. In this way, each of these spreads provides a visual guide to the elements needed to build up a particular type of display.

The first mix features a classic community aquarium of hardy and adaptable fish that will occupy all the available zones and provide easy-care fish keeping for beginners to enjoy. If you have only limited space in your home, the next spread demonstrates that you can still create an interesting and viable display in a compact aquarium. Using a deeper tank gives you the opportunity to keep a range of peaceful and slow-moving species with tall-growing plants that provide sanctuary for them. As a complete contrast, a longer aquarium can play host to a number of active, fast-swimming fish that provide a display of continual movement and interest. If you have space for a generous aquarium, you have the opportunity to establish a community of large and impressive fish. If you are particularly interested in displaying aquarium plants, the next display is based around a wide selection of plants, with fish that will not damage them. The final spread features a community aquarium based around some of the fascinating Rift Valley Lake cichlids.

▲ *Most community fish appreciate a planted tank, although some may damage plants.*

Mixed community aquarium

A mixed community has a little of everything and is a good starting point for new fish keepers. All the fish featured in this example are readily available and will adapt to a wide range of conditions, although as with any aquarium, you should carefully monitor water quality. Since the fish in a mixed community may have differing preferences, try to include a variety of microhabitats in the aquarium design, including open and planted, and provide hiding places, quiet areas, and areas of water movement.

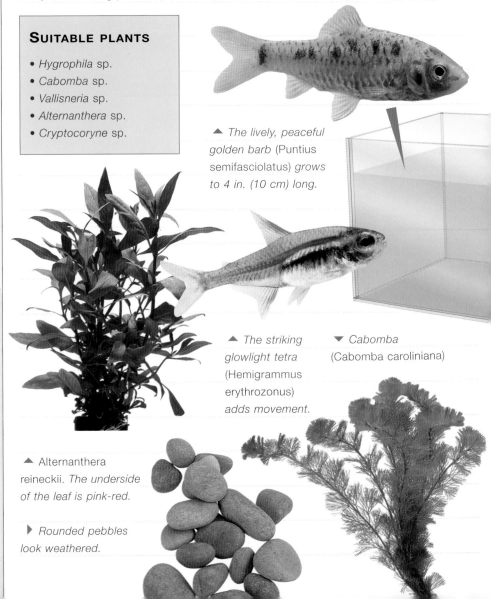

SUITABLE PLANTS

- *Hygrophila* sp.
- *Cabomba* sp.
- *Vallisneria* sp.
- *Alternanthera* sp.
- *Cryptocoryne* sp.

▲ *The lively, peaceful golden barb* (Puntius semifasciolatus) *grows to 4 in. (10 cm) long.*

▲ *The striking glowlight tetra* (Hemigrammus erythrozonus) *adds movement.*

▼ *Cabomba* (Cabomba caroliniana)

▲ Alternanthera reineckii. *The underside of the leaf is pink-red.*

▶ *Rounded pebbles look weathered.*

SUITABLE FISH

- Golden barb
  (Puntius semifasciolatus) x 4
- Platy *(Xiphophorus maculatus)* x 6
- Checkered barb
  (Puntius oligolepis) x 4
- Harlequin rasbora
  (Trigonostigma heteromorpha) x 6

- Zebra danio *(Danio rerio)* x 10
- Zebra loach *(Botia striata)* x 3
- Glowlight tetra
  (Hemigrammus erythrozonus) x 6
- Kribensis *(Pelvicachromis pulcher)* x 2
- Bristlenose plec *(Ancistrus* sp.*)* x 1
- Corydoras catfish *(Corydoras* sp.*)* x 6

Tank dimensions
35 x 18 x 15 in. (90 x 45 x 38 cm)

▼ *Male red wagtail platy (Xiphophorus maculatus)*

▶ *Hygrophila corymbosa is an adaptable aquarium plant.*

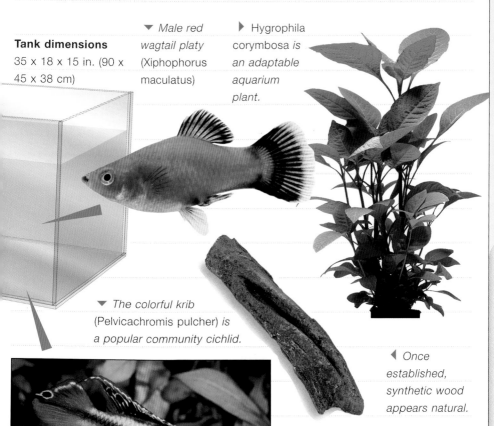

▼ *The colorful krib (Pelvicachromis pulcher) is a popular community cichlid.*

◀ *Once established, synthetic wood appears natural.*

* Take your time when selecting decor for a mixed tank. There are hundreds of items to choose from.

A SMALL AQUARIUM

A small aquarium

Small tanks can be just as interesting as larger displays and are ideal for restricted spaces. Although many fish keepers start with small tanks, these can be trickier to care for than larger ones, since disruptions to the aquarium balance are magnified by the lack of water volume. Carry out maintenance on a little-and-often basis. Live plants provide a good environment for your fish.

SUITABLE PLANTS

- Small *Cryptocoryne* species
- *Salvinia* species
- Creeping Jenny *(Lysimachia nummularia aurea)*
- Java moss *(Vesicularia dubyana)*
- *Hydrocotyle* or *Cardamine* species
- *Lilaeopsis novae-zelandiae*

◀ *The honey gourami (Trichogaster chuna) appreciates dense cover.*

▶ *The threadfin rainbow fish (Iriatherina werneri) shoals in midwater.*

▶ Lilaeopsis novae-zelandiae *spreads across the foreground.*

▼ *Pygmy corydoras (Corydoras pygmaeus)*

▼ Cryptocoryne wendtii *adapts to a wide range of conditions.*

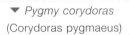

◀ *Mixed grades of gravel on a lime-free base*

SUITABLE FISH

- Threadfin rainbow fish
  (Iriatherina werneri) x 6
- Honey gourami
  (Trichogaster chuna) x 2
- Cherry barb *(Puntius titteya)* x 3
- Clown rasbora
  (Rasbora kalochroma) x 4

- Pygmy corydoras
  (Corydoras pygmaeus) x 6
- Clown plec *(Peckoltia vittata)* x 1
- Japonica/algae shrimps
  (Caridina japonica) x 4
- Siamese fighting fish
  (Betta splendens) x 1

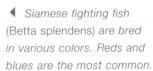

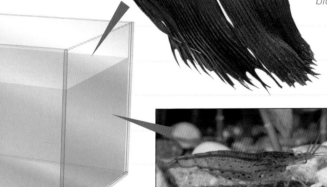

◀ *Siamese fighting fish*
(Betta splendens) *are bred
in various colors. Reds and
blues are the most common.*

** Choose fish
that remain
small in size, and
avoid boisterous
species, since
all your stock
must live in close
proximity.*

▲ *Algae shrimp help
keep the tank clean.*

Tank dimensions
24 x 12 x 12 in.
(60 x 30 x 30 cm)

▼ *Anubias sp.
planted on wood
makes a centerpiece.*

SUITABLE DECOR

- Bogwood with plants attached
  (such as *Anubias*, moss, etc.)
- Small cave (made from stones or
  artificial)
- Silica, lime-free, quartz, or small
  grade substrate
  - Small pebble mix

Peaceful and slow-moving fish

To lose yourself in the tranquillity of the underwater world, avoid choosing boisterous or aggressive fish. The ones featured here have been selected for their presence and peaceful nature, but like many slower-natured fish, they need plenty of hiding spots. Plants, bamboo, and twisted roots provide cover and encourage fish to glide through the aquarium. Tall plants, such as *Vallisneria*, move gently in the flow of water from the filter. Fish that like to hover at the surface appreciate tropical lilies and floating plants.

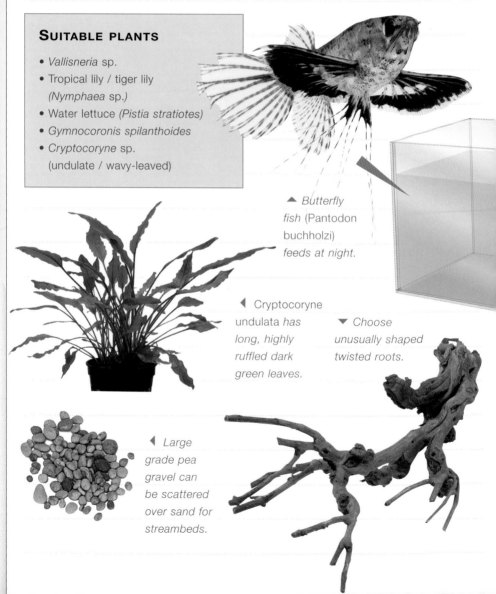

SUITABLE PLANTS

- *Vallisneria* sp.
- Tropical lily / tiger lily *(Nymphaea sp.)*
- Water lettuce *(Pistia stratiotes)*
- *Gymnocoronis spilanthoides*
- *Cryptocoryne* sp. (undulate / wavy-leaved)

▲ *Butterfly fish* (Pantodon buchholzi) *feeds at night.*

◄ Cryptocoryne undulata *has long, highly ruffled dark green leaves.*

▼ *Choose unusually shaped twisted roots.*

◄ *Large grade pea gravel can be scattered over sand for streambeds.*

SUITABLE FISH

- Five-banded barb
  (Puntius pentazona) x 6
- Pearl gourami
  (Trichogaster leeri) x 4
- Moonlight gourami
  (Trichogaster microlepis) x 4
- Brochis sp. *(Brochis splendens)* x 4
- Ram *(Microgeophagus ramirezi)* x 2

- Silver-tip tetra
  (Hasemania nana) x 6
- Spotted headstander
  (Chilodus punctatus) x 4
- Glass catfish
  (Kryptopterus bicirrhis) x 5
- African butterfly fish *(Pantodon buchholzi)* x 2

Tank dimensions
30 x 18 x 12 in.
(75 x 45 x 30 cm)

▶ Vallisneria spiralis *'Tiger'* grows fast in bright light.

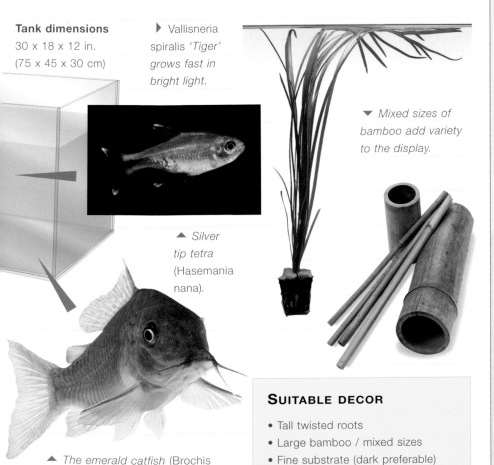

▼ *Mixed sizes of bamboo add variety to the display.*

▲ *Silver tip tetra (Hasemania nana).*

▲ *The emerald catfish (Brochis splendens) is closely related to the true corydoras catfish.*

SUITABLE DECOR

- Tall twisted roots
- Large bamboo / mixed sizes
- Fine substrate (dark preferable)
- Small pebbles / rounded stones

ACTIVE SPECIES

Active species

A lively aquarium with a population of fast-moving fish is great fun to observe. Even if the fish themselves are fairly small, they like to swim and need a long tank with plenty of open spaces. Constant movement requires plenty of oxygen, so water movement and aeration are important. And since many active fish come from clean, streamlike environments, good filtration and plenty of regular water changes are essential. Choose hardy plants, since high oxygen levels remove many plant nutrients from the water.

SUITABLE PLANTS

- Java fern *(Microsorium pteropus)*
- Onion plant *(Crinum thaianum)*
- Cryptocoryne (larger or bulky looking, e.g. *C. pontederiifolia*)
- Amazon sword plant *(Echinodorus* sp.*)*

▲ *Male red wag swordtail* (Xiphophorus helleri).

* Spray bars attached to the filter outlet can distribute water flow over a larger area and help maximize aeration.

▼ *The onion plant (Crinum thaianum) is an adaptable plant.*

▲ *The pictus catfish (Pimelodus pictus) has sharp pectoral fin spines.*

▼ *Westmorland rock has a sandy texture and color.*

* Air pumps can be used to create columns of bubbles throughout the tank, adding to the sense of movement and activity.

SUITABLE FISH

- Swordtail *(Xiphophorus helleri)* x 6
- Lake Kutubu rainbow fish *(Melanotaenia lacustris)* x 4
- Rosy barb *(Puntius conchonius)* x 6
- Longfin, or arulius, barb *(Puntius arulius)* x 4
- Tiger barb *(Puntius tetrazona)* x 10
- Giant danio *(Danio aequipinnatus)* x 6
- Pictus catfish *(Pimelodus pictus)* x 4
- Congo tetra *(Phenacogrammus interruptus)* x 6
- Siamese algae eater *(Crossocheilus siamensis)* x 3

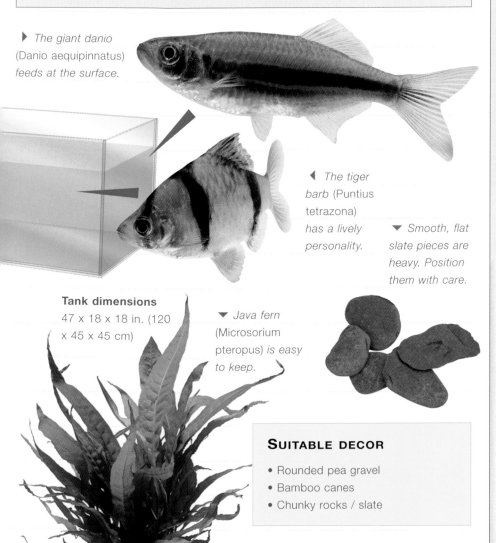

▶ *The giant danio (Danio aequipinnatus) feeds at the surface.*

◀ *The tiger barb (Puntius tetrazona) has a lively personality.*

▼ *Smooth, flat slate pieces are heavy. Position them with care.*

Tank dimensions
47 x 18 x 18 in. (120 x 45 x 45 cm)

▼ *Java fern (Microsorium pteropus) is easy to keep.*

SUITABLE DECOR

- Rounded pea gravel
- Bamboo canes
- Chunky rocks / slate

Large fish

To create a real impact, nothing beats a community of sizable fish. These specimens have distinct characters, which helps to create a bond between them and their owners. Most large fish grow fairly quickly; starting with young fish enables them to get used to each other, thus avoiding conflict, and allows you to watch them develop. Big fish need big tanks, so think seriously before keeping these species; a 71 in. (180 cm) aquarium is a minimum for a community. Many large fish are plant eaters, so live plants are unlikely to survive.

▲ *The severum (Heros severus) is commonly available.*

▼ *The beautiful angel catfish (Synodontis angelicus) emerges at night to feed.*

* Big fish produce an abundance of waste. Only a good external filter, or even two running side by side, will have the capacity to trap and process this material.

ARTIFICIAL PLANTS

If you keep fish that like to dig around or snack on real plants, then artificial plants may be the answer. As they attract a fine coating of algae, the colors begin to tone down, and they will look very realistic.

▲ *Keep single red-tailed black sharks (Epalzeorhynchos bicolor).*

◀ *Mixing light and dark cobbles creates a contrast.*

SUITABLE FISH

- Silver shark
  (Balantiocheilus melanopterus) x 4
- Plecostomus *(Hypostomus sp.)* x 1
- Banded leporinus
  (Leporinus fasciatus) x 1
- Uaru *(Uaru amphiacanthoides)* x 6
- Severum *(Heros severus)* x 4

- Synodontis catfish
  (Synodontis sp.) x 2
- Red-tailed black shark
  (Epalzeorhynchos bicolor) x 1
- Long-nosed distichodus
  (Distichodus lusosso) x 1
- Spanner barb *(Puntius lateristriga)* x 6

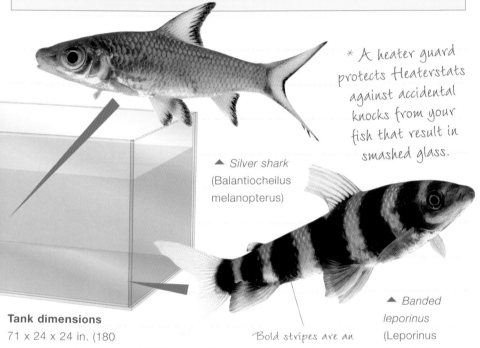

* A heater guard protects Heaterstats against accidental knocks from your fish that result in smashed glass.

▲ Silver shark
(Balantiocheilus
melanopterus)

▲ Banded
leporinus
(Leporinus
fasciatus)

Bold stripes are an attractive feature.

Tank dimensions
71 x 24 x 24 in. (180
x 60 x 60 cm)

▼ *This smooth, two-toned wood is called mopani.*

LARGE FISH

SUITABLE DECOR

- Large bogwood / roots
- Large caves
- Lava rock
- Big cobbles / cobble mix
- Chunky-looking objects

A PLANTED AQUARIUM

A planted aquarium

Care and planning are required when setting up a planted tank, since vital elements, such as the substrate, cannot be easily changed once the aquarium is up and running. For a good display, choose a variety of plant species with contrasting leaf forms and colors, and divide the aquarium into areas for tall, medium, and short plants. Choose the fish on the basis of both their appearance and function. Many scavenging species help to prevent a buildup of mulm, and algae eaters keep plants looking fresh and new.

A simple CO_2 gas fertilization unit will help to promote healthy plant growth.

▶ Barclaya longifolia *stores nutrients in its large corm.*

▼ *The kuhli loach (Pangio kuhlii)* has a *striking pattern.*

SUITABLE PLANTS

- *Ammannia gracilis*
- *Aponogeton sp.*
- *Bacopa sp.*
- *Barclaya longifolia*
- *Eusteralis stellata*
- *Glossostigma elatinoides*
- *Heteranthera zosterifolia*
- *Limnophila aquatica* (Ambulia)
- *Ludwigia sp.*
- *Rotala sp.*
- *Sagittaria sp.*
- *Vallisneria* 'Tiger' (thin-leaved)

The moss will attach to any hard surface and spread in all directions.

◀ Sagittaria platyphylla *has thick leaves.*

▲ *Java moss* (Vesicularia dubyana) *on wood*

SUITABLE FISH

- Golden pencilfish
  (Nannostomus beckfordi) x 6
- Angelfish *(Pterophyllum scalare)* x 6
- Rummy-nose tetra
  (Hemigrammus bleheri) x 10
- Golden panchax
  (Aplocheilus lineatus) x 4

- Japonica shrimp
  (Caridina japonica) x 20
- Otocinclus catfish
  (Otocinclus vittatus) x 6
- Dwarf chain loach
  (Botia sidthimunki) x 4
- Kuhli loach *(Pangio kuhlii)* x 6

Silver sand supports the heating cable and distributes heat evenly.

Lime-free gravel above a nutrient layer.

▲ The angelfish (Pterophyllum scalare) *looks good in a planted aquarium.*

▲ *A substrate heating cable produces currents that move nutrients around plant roots.*

▼ Glossostigma elatinoides

▼ *The small, pale leaves of* Bacopa caroliniana *contrast with other plants.*

Tank dimensions
35 x 18 x 18 in.
(90 x 45 x 45 cm)

SUITABLE DECOR

- Silver sand (if heater cable is used)
- Silica, lime-free, or quartz substrate
- Planting substrate additive / laterite
- Bogwood piece (possibly planted with moss, bolbitis, Java fern, etc.)

African Lake cichlids

The African Lake cichlids are some of the most colorful freshwater fish. To mimic their natural habitat, the essential ingredient is rockwork for the fish to dive through. Since some cichlids can be aggressive, rocks also provide retreats for weaker fish. To protect the heater from knocks, surround it with a guard. There are no plants in this setup since the fish are active plant eaters. They are also messy, so a large external filter with plenty of mechanical sponge media is essential.

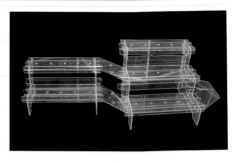

▲ *Reef racks used in marine aquariums make a good foundation for building up lightweight rockscapes.*

▲ *Silver sand looks identical to the type of sand found in many areas of Lake Malawi and makes an ideal substrate for this display.*

Tank dimensions
59 x 18 x 18 in. (150 x 45 x 45 cm)

▶ *For an authentic display, choose large rounded cobbles such as these. Alternatives are lava or tufa rock, which are porous, very light, and easy to stack together.*

▼ *The male zebra cichlid* (Metriaclima zebra) *has egg spots on the tail fin.*

SUITABLE FISH

- Trewavas's cichlid *(Labeotropheus trewavasae)* 1 male, 4 females
- *Melanochromis auratus* 1 male, 2 females
- Zebra cichlid *(Metriaclima sp.)* 4 males of different color forms, 12 females

▼ *Labeotropheus trewavasae has many color forms.*

▲ *Melanochromis auratus has bold horizontal stripes.*

Smooth ocean rock is suitable for this setup.

Calcareous oceanic rock will help maintain pH levels.

SUITABLE DECOR

- Big cobbles
- Lava rock
- Ocean or tufa rock
- Coral gravel
- Silver sand

AFRICAN LAKE CICHLIDS

Picture credits

Additional picture credits

The publishers would like to thank the following photographers for providing images, credited here by page number and position: T (Top), B (Bottom), C (Center), BL (Bottom left), etc.

Aqua Press (M-P & C. Piednoir): 39, 45(TL), 55(BR), 58(TL), 59(TL), 67(BL), 69(BL), 72(BL), 74(TL), 75(CR), 76(BR), 83(B)

Neil Hepworth: 61(BL)

Peter Hiscock: 75(BL)

Jan-Eric Larsson-Rubenowitz: 95(TR)

The information and recommendations in this book are given without any guarantees on the part of the author and publisher, who disclaim any liability with the use of this material.